Sanitized Apartheid

Education, Culture, and Society

The titles published in this series are listed at *brill.com/ecas*

Sanitized Apartheid

*The Post-Racial Hoax in South Africa and
the United States*

By

Arnold Dodge

BRILL

SENSE

LEIDEN | BOSTON

All chapters in this book have undergone peer review.

The Library of Congress Cataloging-in-Publication Data is available online at http://catalog.loc.gov

Typeface for the Latin, Greek, and Cyrillic scripts: "Brill". See and download: brill.com/brill-typeface.

ISSN 2590-0005
ISBN 978-90-04-44442-3 (paperback)
ISBN 978-90-04-39122-2 (hardback)
ISBN 978-90-04-44443-0 (e-book)

This book is printed on acid-free paper and produced in a sustainable manner.

Contents

Preface

In the chapters that follow, I attempt to expose the canard that citizens in South Africa and the United States have left their racialized visions of the world behind them. I share many of my own experiences, as they relate to the themes of the book, as I journeyed through schools, towns, and neighborhoods in both countries over a 12-year period. During these visits I have had extensive conversations with people from all walks of life – educators, school children, shopkeepers, suburban parents, township parents, police officers, attorneys, laborers – journaling and recording, as appropriate. I have interacted with them in both professional and social settings.

In my 50 years in education, I have held many positions, including teacher, principal, superintendent and professor/chair of a university education department. I have participated in educational forums throughout the United States and in several international assemblies of educational leaders. In this book I will rely on many of the researchers who have studied the racial divide. I take the liberty of including their viewpoints in the presentation.

I will also share stories from my biography – independent of my professional life – which I hope will deepen the intimacy between writer and reader. I connect my personal discoveries to the reading and research I have conducted on the examined areas. I submit reflections from others (whom I have met along the way) on the subjects of race, class, schooling and social intersections, to enrich the conversation. Quite often I raise questions for which I do not have answers. On this last point I wish to emphasize that I do not consider myself an authority on the subject of the racial divide. I do, however, have an abiding interest – and passion – for discovering more about the phenomenon.

To my friends in both the United States and South Africa, let me offer apologies from the start. I have tried to do my level best to accurately depict the conditions I have observed in my travels throughout the regions in your countries, ones that I use as the platform for the discussion. I may not have succeeded on some (many?) occasions. I do not pretend to fully understand the history and the social dynamics that make your home what it is. Instead, I offer this book as an attempt to reveal disparities in the social/cultural/educational environments that I have uncovered in my investigation. To this end I hope to stimulate frank dialogue, and where appropriate, make change.

Throughout the book, I share stories that are intimate and painful, not only for me, but for the people I refer to at times. (Note that I have striven to keep anonymous all others referenced in conversations and other exchanges.) I believe it necessary to include these observations in the narrative since they bear witness to the dysfunctions under examination. I take full responsibility for the choices made regarding the tone and the substance of the material presented. In that vein, let me add that I regard the project as, in part, auto-ethnographic. I attempt to connect the personal and the political with the goal of disrupting complacent perspectives – including my own – on matters of race. In doing so, I hope to meet the standards for auto-ethnography, a most potent delivery system for portraits of social abuse. My hope is that the reader will experience discomfort, a discomfort that may lead to a new awareness. This is not an easy undertaking.

I invite you to join me in the struggle.

Acknowledgements

Thanks to my colleague, counterpart, and friend, Professor Berte van Wyk of Stellenbosch University. His focus on dismantling the scourge of racism is a mission fueled by hope, setting an example for others to follow.

With a deep sense of gratitude and respect I acknowledge all the teachers and administrators who invited us into their classrooms and schools in both South Africa and the US. The abundance of compassion and love they have for the students in their charge has been an inspiration.

I thank my family and friends for their patience and encouragement as I slogged through the travails of writing.

Finally, I thank those I met along the way who shared the hard truths about a world in need of healing.

CHAPTER 1

Sanitized Apartheid

Sanitized: made less offensive by eliminating anything unwholesome, objectionable, incriminating, etc.

Apartheid: a system or practice that separates people according to color, ethnicity, caste, etc.

As I walked – and crawled – through the cave passages, I bravely ignored my claustrophobia. Pushing through the fear paid off. Buried deep within the cave walls and floor, were the bones of the first human beings to walk the planet. Signs indicated where the remains were found and the estimated time-period of the civilization that lived there. The tour guide was casual. I was dumbstruck.

I was in the Cradle of Humankind, a World Heritage site not far from Johannesburg, South Africa, renowned as the location of humankind's origins. The center focuses on the development of the human family over millions of years. In 1924, the first hominid, Australopithecus, was discovered here. The Sterkfontein Caves, occupying one section of the site, is the longest and most continuous paleoanthropological excavation in the world. These caves' fossil finds include the pre-human skull of "Mrs. Ples" and the complete skeleton of "Little Foot." The tour included an historical overview tracing the origins of the human species.

During my visit, I learned things that not only changed my view of the world, but changed my view of myself. As I made my way out of the museum grounds, I had a breathtaking revelation:

The first human beings came from Africa! My ancestors are African! I am a descendant of Black people! I must be Black! But I'm not Black. What happened?

It's complicated.

In this book I share my experiences in a journey to uncover the mysteries of racial oppression. In this quest, I interact with communities in South Africa and the United States – with educators, students, shopkeepers, friends, and others; sometimes in topic-focused discussions, at other times simply mingling. I also unpack my own history and viewpoints on racial issues. I attempt to weave historical and theoretical perspectives into the narrative. I believe this mixture of

© KONINKLIJKE BRILL NV, LEIDEN, 2020 | DOI: 10.1163/9789004444430_001

the personal and the referential provides powerful fuel to propel the excursion. I ask the reader to bear with me as I shift gears on the ride.

1   The (Very) First Great Migration

1.1   *The Color Palette Begins*

Why do some people have dark skin and others light skin? And why, in so many instances, do people of similar skin color cluster together in regions around the world? The science behind the phenomenon is explained on the Smithsonian National Museum of Natural History website, in a section entitled "Modern Human Diversity – Skin Color."

> As early humans moved into hot, open environments in search of food and water, one big challenge was keeping cool. The adaptation that was favored involved an increase in the number of sweat glands on the skin while at the same time reducing the amount of body hair. With less hair, perspiration could evaporate more easily and cool the body more efficiently. But this less-hairy skin was a problem because it was exposed to a very strong sun, especially in lands near the equator. Since strong sun exposure damages the body, the solution was to evolve skin that was permanently dark so as to protect against the sun's more damaging rays.
>
> Melanin, the skin's brown pigment, is a natural sunscreen that protects tropical peoples from the many harmful effects of ultraviolet (UV) rays. UV rays can, for example, strip away folic acid, a nutrient essential to the development of healthy fetuses. Yet when a certain amount of UV rays penetrates the skin, it helps the human body use vitamin D to absorb the calcium necessary for strong bones. This delicate balancing act explains why the peoples that migrated to colder geographic zones with less sunlight developed lighter skin color. As people moved to areas farther from the equator with lower UV levels, natural selection favored lighter skin which allowed UV rays to penetrate and produce essential vitamin D. The darker skin of peoples who lived closer to the equator was important in preventing folate deficiency.[1]

As our ancestors migrated north they took different routes. While there are many theories as to how these migrations took place, there is consensus on some issues. The first group out of Africa left the continent 60,000 to 70,000 years ago. They journeyed through the Middle East via the Arabian Peninsula. From there, the path led to Asia, Europe and the Indian subcontinent. It was thought that primitive boats and rafts were used to cross the seas for those who would take up residence in Australia. The bridge to the new world, aka North and South America, was formed by the joint land mass that at one time connected Siberia and Alaska.

1.2   *Tribal Identities Emerge*

While adaptations to climate changes are markers of physical differences, the arc of human history is also explained through a social, cultural, and political lens, which reveals an extraordinarily complex dynamic spanning tens of thousands of years. As groups merged in the ever-burgeoning human population, communities were formed. Tribes, hoards, and other collectives developed common languages as they moved about to efficiently exploit resources, which were abundant in some areas and scarce in others. Conflict began over these resources. Fortified boundaries were established to protect communities. The powerful overtook and expropriated resources from the less powerful and subjugated their weaker counterparts, forcing them into slavery or, in some cases, slaughter. As travel became elaborated, oceans were traversed and conquest took on a global reach.

The way we look is a product of a biological imperative to survive. By accident of birth we land on the planet with a skin tone inherited from our ancestors who migrated to safer spaces to avoid extinction. Today's iteration of the human diaspora divides up the world into a crazy quilt of colors, some places with high concentrations of darker skinned people, others with concentrations of lighter skinned people, and still others with mixed populations. Two such locations, South Africa and the United States, are examined in this book for how they have faced the challenges of racial compositions that often roil the public weal.

2   South Africa, Land of Opportunity

2.1   *From Way Station to Permanent Address*

South Africa, the southernmost country in Africa and the 25th largest country in the world, has an inglorious history of various groups claiming they are the rightful occupants of land. It is a tumultuous, torturous, and hard-to-follow stream of events.

The Bantu, Khoisan, Xhosa, and Zulu peoples were prominently featured in tribal histories – they were the original residents of the region. European contact began in the late 1400s. Over the course of several hundred years, the English, Dutch, and Portuguese found a visit to South Africa to be most advantageous. One reason was the Cape of Good Hope. As the southernmost point in all of Africa, it became the favorite place for ships to stock up as they traveled on trade routes between Europe and Asia. In fact, Jan van Riebeeck, on behalf of the Dutch East India Company, set up a "refreshment" stand at the Cape, replete with fruit to battle the scurvy that threatened the lives of the voyagers.

During the early 1800s, Dutch, Flemish, German, and French settlers (aka the "Boers") and the English claimed land in the north and east of the country. Cape Town was the site of settlements of French Huguenots who were fleeing religious persecution in their home country. Dutch settlers, forebears of the Afrikaaners, first arrived in the 17th and 18th centuries. The Indian segment of the population came mostly from the slave trade between Indian Muslim rulers and the Dutch from the 1860s onward.

Wars were fought on many frontiers. There was a series of conflicts between the Dutch and Khoisan people in the 1600s. The English fought the Xhosa peoples and then annexed Cape Colony. The discovery of diamonds and gold in the mid-1800s intensified European efforts to gain control over indigenous people. The Zulus fought – and lost – a war with the British. During the first Boer War (1880–1881), the Boer Republics defeated British encroachments. During the second Boer War (1899–1902), the British prevailed.

2.2   *The Re-Structuring of the Social/Cultural Architecture by the Colonial Overlords*

The British parliament created the Union of South Africa in 1910, granting nominal independence to the region. In 1913, the Land Act reserved 90% of the country for Whites. Strikes, protests, and changes in leadership marked the periods from the First World War through the Great Depression and to the end of the Second World War.

In 1948, the National Party was elected to power which strengthened segregation under British and Dutch rule. The country was officially classified into four races – a system known as apartheid, which one South African president called "good neighborliness" (Oneale, 2013). Pass cards were issued that described a person's status – Black, Coloured,[2] Indian, or White. The African National Congress (ANC) would end up doing battle with the National Party for over 40 years to undo apartheid ideology.

The 1950s saw additional repressive laws put into place, including the Group Areas Act, which forbade different groups from living with one another. The pass laws, also known as the natives law, severely limited the movements of not only Black African citizens, but other people as well, by requiring them to carry pass books when outside their homelands or designated areas.

In 1961, the country became a republic and left the Commonwealth. PW Botha's Constitution Act of 1983 reaffirmed the policy of apartheid. The 1960s through the 1990s were filled with crises that shook the nation repeatedly. Major resistance was led by the ANC, the group whose leadership included Nelson Mandela, who ended up with a life sentence for his participation. In 1990, Mandela was released from prison. Apartheid was dismantled as official government policy in 1991. In 1993, President FW de Klerk opened bilateral discussions with Mandela. In 1994, the first democratic elections were held and Nelson Mandela was elected President.

2.3 *Apartheid Is Abolished, the Legacy of Containment Continues*
Despite the official dismantling of apartheid 25 years ago, Black and Brown people remain marginalized in South Africa. Despite the advent of massive political shifts, including a small minority of Black citizens becoming wealthy and occupying leadership positions, the vast majority of Black and Brown people are still waiting for the rewards of freedom. Notably, data from a recent study (Pariona, 2019) show the breakdown of ethnic groups: 80.5% Black, 8.8% Coloured, 8.3% White and, 2.5% Indian and Asian.

One South African educator, a former principal and current practicing staff developer, said much of the political conversation is still about apartheid and its lingering effects on the traditionally disenfranchised. There are attempts to right the imbalances; however, they are often misguided or ineffective. He points to the Black Economic Empowerment (BEE) movement, which is a formal repudiation of apartheid. This initiative, codified in 2001, is designed to address economic inequalities that still exist in the country. It seeks to redistribute the management and control of South Africa's financial resources to the majority of the country. By doing so, BEE's intention is to increase participation in decision making in the Black, Coloured, and Asian communities. (It is worth noting the BEE has had its critics and has yielded mixed results at best since its inception.)

The gaps are getting worse. As I have made my way throughout the Western Cape over the years, I have witnessed first-hand the landscapes that testify to these disparities.

A glaring example of the subaltern class distinction is the township, a large tract of land that contain shacks, most of which do not have running water or electric power. Khayelitsha, one of the largest townships, has over 500,000 residents living on 10,000/km^2 of land, or just over 30,000 people per square mile. As a visitor makes his way from parts east on the N2 highway to Cape Town proper, the Khayelitsha landscape seems to go on forever, tens of thousands of corrugated metal huts piled upon one another like strewn refuse. Arriving in Cape Town, just a few minutes past the township, the traveler is greeted by a city replete with five star hotels, a waterfront, boutique-style shopping area, and magnificent hilltop homes.

Hard as it is to fathom, the "informal settlement," as it is known, is a bleaker housing arrangement on the South African landscape than the township. These areas are often illegally built on municipal land. Langrug is one of these settlements located in the village of Franschhoek. It is home to at least 5,000 people who live in 2,000 shacks. It was originally created by migrants looking for job opportunities in the early 1990s. Langrug suffers from lack of running water and electricity, poor sanitation, and little or no access to health care or other human services. Yet, Franschoek is also home to 52 wineries, which overlook some of the most beautiful mountain scenery in the world and serve top shelf wines to patrons visiting from around the world. I visit such wineries during my stays and the experience is elegant and upscale, rivaling the finest tourist venues in the world.

On one of my trips, I was in a taxi driving past Alexandra, regarded by many as the most notorious and dangerous township in all of South Africa. I ventured into this township on one of my visits. The conditions were deplorable, some of the worst I had seen in any of my trips. The taxi then passed a hotel/casino complex. I stopped in. The luxury was undeniable. The complex was not more than 10 minutes from the township. As if this extreme contrast is not enough, Alexandra's next-door neighbor is Sandton, one of the richest and most exclusive areas in all of Africa. (More details on Alexandra and Sandton are discussed in chapter three.)

Driving through the South African countryside, one comes upon Black and Coloured townships and White enclaves. As I have made my way through various sections of the country, I learned to surmise – from a distance – the color of the skin of people occupying different communities that I passed on the highways. The most dilapidated, neglected, and crowded housing areas were typically populated by Black people. Those areas that seemed to be better taken care of, less crowded, generally more appealing, were typically occupied by Coloured people. Homes in communities occupied by White people were clearly respectable and upscale places – reminiscent, in fact, of wealthy condominium communities in the suburbs of the United States.

3   America, the New Frontier

3.1   *Conquering the Natives*

Those to first cross the Bering Land Bridge eventually spread out through what is today the western United States, with many moving on to settle in the Southern Hemisphere. Native Americans were the first to cultivate the land, form productive communities, and develop various languages and customs. Some became skilled farmers, others hunted sea mammals from boats and caught fish with ingenious methods. Nation states were established and trading flourished among them.

And then came the Europeans.

Christopher Columbus opened the "New World" franchise with his voyage in 1492. The settlers brought with them diseases, including smallpox and measles, that wiped out whole Native American villages. (Most of the settlers themselves had developed immunities to the diseases.) The invaders began to expropriate farmland for crops and jobs for the growing European settlements. The colonizers often fought with the indigenous population having the upper hand because of their guns, which overpowered the Natives' less technologically advanced weapons. As ghastly a truth as it is, the Nazis idolized America's approach to the natives (Ross, 2018). Hitler remarked, approvingly, that White settlers in America had "gunned down the millions of redskins to a few hundred thousand." When he spoke of Lebensraum, the German drive for living space in Eastern Europe, he often had America in mind.[3] As Ross (2018) suggests, American history is rife with precedents to capture the fiendish imagination. Thomas Jefferson spoke of the need to "eliminate" or "extirpate" Native Americans. In 1856, an Oregonian settler wrote, "Extermination, however unchristianlike it may appear, seems to be the only resort left for the protection of life and property." General Philip Sheridan spoke of "annihilation, obliteration, and complete destruction" (Ross, 2018). While many tribal nations resisted the incursion, eventually they were forced to surrender their lands and were moved to reservations.

3.2   *Importing the Africans*

Slavery in America began in the early 1600s and lasted 250 years. The need to produce tobacco – and later cotton – was the engine that kept the slave trade moving. People were kidnapped from their African homelands and forced aboard ships to become "slaves" to their "masters." The Middle Passage – common parlance for the Trans-Atlantic slave trade – is notorious for many reasons, including the conditions of slave transport, wherein thousands died of starvation, disease, asphyxiation, and of other things in unspeakable conditions in the hulls of ships. It is estimated that between 10 and 15 million enslaved Africans arrived on the shores of America and that a similar number perished along the way (DeGruy, 2005).

The American zeitgeist somehow made peace with the notion that other people were inferior based on their appearance, going so far as to endorse slavery in the Constitution. Bizarre rationales were employed to support this perspective. The historian Sander Gilman whose work, in part, focuses on medicine in social and political discourse, shares this bit of cultural treachery:

> Medical tradition has a long history of perceiving this skin color as the result of some pathology. The favorite theory, which reappears with some frequency in the early nineteenth century, is that the skin color and attendant physiognomy of the Black are the result of congenital leprosy. (DeGruy, 2005, p. 78)

DeGruy (2005) weighs in with this indictment:

> In few societies, if any, were so large a group of people considered to be less than human based upon physical appearance. Yet Europeans concluded that Black Africans were fitted by a natural act of God to the position of permanent bondage. It was this relegation to lesser humanity that allowed the institution of chattel slavery to be intrinsically linked with violence, and it was through violence, aggression, and dehumanization that the institution of slavery was enacted, legislated, and perpetuated by Europeans. (pp. 48–49)

As with other crimes against humanity, American slavery was a deformity of the body politic. And, as Stephanie Smallwood, a researcher on the Middle Passage, says, although the images of the abominable trek across the sea are associated with the symbolism of shackles, we shouldn't lose a more nuanced understanding of the human cost, namely, the "social violence of being separated from your entire genealogy in Africa" (Ryzik, 2016, p. 28).

Several milestones in the mid-1800s reflect the disparate public policy positions regarding slavery. In the Dred Scott decision in 1857, the United States Supreme Court said "Negroes" were not citizens and therefore had no right to citizenship. Slaves that escaped their masters remained "property" of their owners and had to be returned. In 1860, Abraham Lincoln, a member of the Republican Party, at the time opposed to slavery, was elected President. Southern states seceded from the union largely because of the contentiousness around slavery. A civil war ensued. In 1863, Lincoln issued the Emancipation Proclamation which changed the legal status of enslaved African Americans in the Confederate states from slave to free.

The 13th Amendment was ratified by Congress in 1856, constitutionally abolishing slavery as an institution. In the aftermath of the North's victory in the Civil War – and despite the imprimatur of constitutional equality – the victimization of people of color morphed into a thousand spokes, driving the wheels of racist acts and intentions.

3.3   *Jim Crow Carries on the Dirty Work*

Eric Williams, a Trinidadian politician and historian, asserts that "Slavery was not born of racism; rather racism was the consequence of slavery."[4] Williams' claim seems accurate in light of America's infamy regarding the treatment of former slaves after emancipation. The next generation of abuse directed at people of color was a relentless pursuit of non-citizenship and non-entitlement to the fruits of society. Many would assert that this ethos towards people of color in the US has remained intact, especially through the mid-20th century.

The fictional character "Jim Crow" was popularized by a minstrel show performance in the 1830s which featured a caricature of a clumsy and simple-minded Black slave. The show was a huge success, White audiences in both the US and Great Britain gleefully enjoying the blackface and the slave dialect. The phrase was appropriated in the late 19th century as a term to describe anti-Black laws after Reconstruction, such as those instituting restrictions on voting rights (including required literacy tests), bans on interracial relation-ships, and permission for businesses to separate their Black and White clien-tele. "Separate but equal" offered a license for racial division. Codified by the US Supreme Court (in *Plessy v. Ferguson*), the new doctrine allowed for wide-spread segregated public spaces and services, including railroad cars, bath-rooms, water fountains, and ... schools.

Racial animus and outright bigotry were part and parcel of community and political life in shockingly public examples in the first half of the 20th century. The thought leaders of this period – politicians, journalists, and others – pro-vided the signals for continuing the American racial division.

Woodrow Wilson, 28th President of the United States, was the shepherd of progressive legislative policies, leader of the United States through World War I, and champion of an active foreign policy agenda known as "Wilsonianism." This included the grand Fourteen Points – which helped establish the League of Nations that would achieve an enduring peace in the world. This very same statesman expressed pride that during his tenure as Princeton University Pres-ident no African Americans were admitted. He was supportive of the KKK's mission – even willing to forgive their terror tactics. He showed the movie *Birth of a Nation*, an infamous tale of heroic Klansmen, in the White House in 1915 (Evers, 2015; Gates, 2019). Wilson once called racial segregation "a benefit" and defended the enslavement of Blacks, suggesting that "The domestic slaves, at any rate, and almost all who were much under the master's eye, were happy and well cared for."[5]

Franklin Delano Roosevelt, whose leadership provided a bulwark against fascism, had no interest in dialogue with Black journalists from what was known as the "Negro Press" during his time in office. An alarming domestic issue of the day for Blacks was the government's decision to separate enlisted men and women by race, even going so far as to separate plasma in the wartime blood bank (Staples, 2016). Roosevelt kept his distance from those wanting to question him about these policies. His interest, ironically, was in saving the world from a tyrant who espoused a "master race" philosophy.

With regard to journalistic responsibility on matters related to race during the first half of the 20th century, Flournoy (2012) cites the mainstream press – in a harsh rebuke – for its lack of reporting on the "humiliation and horror inflicted on African American's in the Jim Crow South" (p. 4).

> From east to west, newspapers ignored Black Americans. Studies of the *New York Times* covering 1900 to 1953 found that, except for isolated instances, the *Times* devoted no more than 1% of its average daily content to Black Americans. There was one exception: crime. In 1949, the Southern Regional Council examined more than 1,000 stories in mainstream Southern newspapers and found almost no mention of African Americans unless they'd allegedly committed a crime. The work of the 1946–1947 class of Nieman fellows at Harvard University found evidence of this on a national scale. At the end of a year-long study, this remarkable group concluded, 'North and South, most newspapers are consistently cruel to the colored man, patronizing him, keeping him in his place, thoughtlessly crucifying him in a thousand big and little ways.' As pictured in many newspapers, the Negro is either an 'entertaining fool, a dangerous animal, or ... a prodigy of astonishing attainments, considering his race.' (Flournoy, 2012, p. 4)

Another dreadful footnote in America's story is linked once again to the Nazis. Hitler not only admired the way the United States handled Native Americans, he approved of the very principles, the cornerstone, perhaps, of the racist society that was on display in America: "... the Nazis took inspiration from American racism of the late nineteenth and twentieth centuries ... in 'Mein Kampf,' Hitler praises America as the one state that has made progress toward a primarily racial conception of citizenship, by excluding certain races from naturalization" (Ross, 2018).

The Jim Crow cloud began to dissipate in the latter part of the 20th century and in the first decades of the 21st century; however, the American people still find ingenious ways to cast a shadow on racial equality. People in the US have learned that if they want to practice racism, they have to clean up their act. The Jim Crow approach needs a makeover, i.e., the racial divide needs to go undercover if it is too succeed; it has to be "dressed up" when seen in public. Somehow, through a cultural sleight of hand, we have been able to convince one another that we have grown past the racialized versions of ourselves. While there remain instances of overt and aggressive racism, most would contend we're over it. Racism has, in fact, gone underground, like a stream polluting the land. Sometimes it may be hard to detect, but its influence is always toxic.

4   Normalizing Depredation

> Perhaps the sentiments contained in the following pages are not yet sufficiently fashionable to procure them general favor; a long habit of not thinking a thing wrong gives it a superficial appearance of being right and raises at first a formidable outcry in defence [sic] of custom. But tumult soon subsides. Time makes more converts than reason. (Opening passage from Thomas Paine's *Common Sense*)

The normalization of racism in both South Africa and the United States continues apace. (Despite Paine's dictum, time seems to have failed in its conversion mission with regard to racism.) Most are eager to normalize conditions that currently exist, despite evidence that things remain unbalanced. Many who would espouse the new equality, boast about how far their countries have come.

Turner (2015) takes on the challenge of unpacking US school districts' responses to demographic shifts – in race, class, and immigration. "Meaning making" by school district leaders involves an interpretation of a situation that is socially contextualized and therefore open to multiple viewpoints.

> The use of language and symbolism is central to meaning-making. In particular, frames – 'specific metaphors, symbolic representations, and cognitive cues' (Zald, 1996, p. 262, as cited in Turner, 2015, p. 7) – connect with people's existing knowledge, values, and beliefs in ways that simplify, condense, and organize events and make them meaningful. Frames focus attention on some aspects of a situation and direct attention away from others. (Benford & Snow, 2000; Stone, 2002, as cited in Turner, 2015, p. 7)

Hannah Arendt's characterization of Adolph Eichmann, the architect of the gas chamber in Nazi Germany, comes to mind (Arendt, 1963). Eichmann, she said, was just another common man performing what he thought was his duty.

He was not evil, he was engaged in activities that had become normalized in society. As distressing as this analogy may be – and perhaps, for some, too extreme – it is instructive as one examines the ongoing inequalities that exist in both South Africa and the United States and the social engines that keep them going.

The campaign to distort reality regarding racial divisions is outlined by Harris (2012). Using Critical Race Theory[6] as a benchmark, she has outlined the tenets of a society where racism is baked in and, therefore, often ignored. (References to South Africa and the US have been added for context.)

- Racism persists despite its nearly universal condemnation by state policy and by the norms of "polite" society.
- Racism is ordinary and normal in South African/US society.
- Formal legal equality has produced only modest success in improving the lived experience of most people of color.
- Domination can exist without coercion.
- Existing anti-discrimination laws omit the perspective of the racially subordinated.
- Legal perspectives are aligned with White privilege.
- De jure segregation and de facto segregation have contributed to racial isolation.
- Striking down de jure segregation in schools has become an historical artifact – without contemporary significance – given the re-segregation of US schools/the continuing segregation of South African schools.
- There appears to be an "intersectionality" when exploring bias related to race, ethnicity, religion, national origin, class, and sexuality.
- The traditional focus on racism's victims leaves unexamined the everyday ways in which persons who are not victimizers benefit from racial hierarchies.

4.1   Playing the Obama Card

Many in the US will suggest that, of course, we are now "normal," our racialized past behind us. We elected a Black president! What more do you want?

As pointed out by Muhammad (2017), Obama's presidency represented the "highest expression of the goal of assimilation." However, the Obama years were also a lesson in how Black leadership alone is not the antidote to the "gaping wounds of racial injustice in America." Muhammad (2017) continues:

> We now live in a post-assimilation America. The 50-year-old rules for racial advancement are obsolete. There is no racial barrier left to break. There is no office in the land to which an African-American can ascend –

from mayor to attorney general and the presidency – that will serve as a magical platform for saving Black people and our nation's soul from its racist past. We cannot engineer a more equitable nation simply by dressing up institutions in more shades of Brown. Instead, we must confront structural racism and the values of our institutions. (SR 5)

4.2   *Race and Class*

The lack of educational opportunities for township children in South Africa is particularly disturbing. Education during apartheid was designed, in part, to keep the society racially divided. As noted by Constas (1996), things may not have changed all that much post-apartheid.

> As is well known, education in South Africa was an integral part of the plan to build and maintain the system of apartheid ... educational policies were designed ... specifically to ensure political, economic, and social domination of one racial group over others .... Despite South Africa's transition into what has been termed a "postapartheid era," efforts to develop an equitable system of education continue to be hindered by fiscal inequalities and political violence. The disaster of South African education can be brought into sharp focus by considering the material inequalities of schooling and the broad social decay created by apartheid. (p. 683)

Constas' comments were made over 20 years ago. However, his perspectives on the situation continued to appear in the public conversation. Spaull (2015) opines:

> ... poor school performance in South Africa reinforces social inequality: children inherit the social station of their parents, irrespective of their own motivation or ability. Until such times as the Department of Basic Education and the ruling administration are willing to seriously address the underlying issues in education, at whatever political or economic cost, the existing patterns of underperformance and inequality will continue unabated. (p. 21)

The message here is unsurprising to a public that has become inured to the narrative that inequalities still abound in all facets of contemporary South Africa – and may be inevitable.

In the United States, conditions between well-resourced schools and under-resourced schools are also stark. In addition, the (relatively) recent focus on standardized test scores – and their announcement to the public – makes a particularly insidious contribution to normalization. In this regard, Sonya Douglass Horsford (Bass, 2014) reflects on progress made 60 years after *Brown v. Board of Education*. She references the categories established by the Federal Education Act of 2004, commonly known as No Child Left Behind, categories which continue to inform the newer federal programs and legislation such as Race to the Top and the Every Student Succeeds Act.

> I think, while data are useful in showing us where we are as educators, and that researchers should target our focus in supporting all students, I think data also have become used as kind of an explanation or way of normalizing failure for Blacks and students in poverty and other students that we continue to see at the bottom of the "achievement gap." (Horsford, as cited in Bass, 2014, p. 20)[7]

Horsford's point is abundantly evinced in regular reporting in the US press of student test scores by school district. Displays of test scores in Long Island schools have become predictable. Where there are large populations of Black and Brown children, test scores are well below the median. This regular reminder of poor achievement for certain groups reinforces the storyline.

Normalization is a fiendish – and powerful – tool. As Boomer (1992) points out, "… individual action is usually contained and rendered ineffectual when it begins to threaten the established order" (p. 8). Many of good conscience have formed organizations that have acted as agents of social justice by calling out normalization of racism when they see it. One way they push back is to keep an energized, focused, and courageous conversation going. In order to do so, the master narrative – based on a willful ignorance of the facts – must be challenged. Counter narratives – based on reality – need to be articulated. The South African and US contexts provide plenty of grist for the counter narrative mill, particularly around educational issues.

While it is true that laws and regulations have been cleaned up so as to appear as a lever for justice for all, White economic and political power dominates social infrastructures. In fact, an insidious version of racism now exists in both South Africa and the United States whereby those in power claim they don't see color, merit is all that matters, those who have more are always ready to help those who have less, segregation has been outlawed and, therefore, where people live, send their children to school, etc., are matters of choice. As Harris (2012) points out, in the US, there exists a "collective denial" that serves to justify racist motives and practices. By adopting the convenient lie that they are post-racial, many in South Africa and the US are ready to move on.

The current project is designed to slow things down for a more critical look.

Notes

1 Retrieved from https://humanorigins.si.edu/evidence/genetics/human-skin-color-variation/modern-human-diversity-skin-color

2 The word "Coloured" is presented here in the spelling common during the apartheid era and is used throughout the book as it appears within an apartheid categorization context.

3 Additional disturbing quotes on Hitler's admiration for flashpoints in American history and precedents that may have substantiated his perspective can be found in Ross, Alex. "How American Racism Influenced Hitler." *The New Yorker*, 30 April 2018. Retrieved from https://www.newyorker.com/magazine/2018/04/30/how-american-racism-influenced-hitler

4 Williams' quote is highlighted in a stunning piece on the unholy alliance between slavery, capitalism, and White supremacy, *The Roots of Racism*, by Lance Selfa, retrieved from https://socialistworker.org/2010/10/21/the-roots-of-racism

5 Retrieved from https://thelibertarianrepublic.com/top-10-racist-quotes-progressive-hero-woodrow-wilson/
Top 10 Most Racist Quotes from Progressive Hero Woodrow Wilson.

6 For an in-depth study of Critical Race Theory, see Taylor, Gillborn, and Ladson-Billings (2009).

7 Horsford has authored a powerful treatise on education reform in the post-Civil Rights era, *Learning in a Burning House: Educational Inequality, Ideology, and (Dis) Integration.*

CHAPTER 2

Skin in the Game

In stores downtown, they follow me because I'm Brown.
JAQUELINE WOODSON (Poet)

∴

The implications of separating people based on race, whether by law or custom, are profound. From birth, human beings are hyper-reactive to prompts in their environment. This is especially true for those whom we meet as we first enter the world.

> By three months of age [babies] ... stare longer at a face from their own racial group than at one from a less familiar racial group ... Babies will always tend to gravitate to sensory information they have been exposed to before, preferring it to sights, sounds, and other sensory inputs that are unfamiliar and strange. . . By nine months of age infants are better able to tell two own-race faces apart compared to two other-race faces ... The failure to discriminate within an unfamiliar category is such a well-documented phenomenon that it has a name in the psychological litera-ture: the 'out-group homogeneity effect.' (Banaji & Greenwald, 2016)

There is evidence of growth potential in this skill as well. Exposing the infant to just three instances of out-group faces enhances out-group sensitivity. In other words, even brief encounters can expand the repertoire. Of course, the opposite is true. The more prolonged the absence of out-groups in the field of perception, the more bewildered the response when the out-group stimulus does appear.

1 The "Other"

We begin to formulate a mental model of "the other" for those with whom we are unfamiliar. The characterization of those who look different than we do – or have different traditions, customs, and language – is dependent to a large measure on our interactions with them. One of the unfortunate outcomes of minimal interactions is that significant social and cultural assumptions are made about others, most of them counterfeit. Left to our own devices – and with the inheritance of bias – ugly, mean, and sometimes violent behavior becomes directed towards those we see as different. The 20th century Austrian philosopher Martin Buber comes to mind in this human dilemma. Buber characterized a relation between two "subjects" as I/thou. He characterized a relation between a subject and an object as I/it. In the first instance, there is an equality, a mutuality that exists in the relationship. In the second, there is control and an expectation that the "it" will be passive. The "other" becomes the "it" in Buber's equation (Buber, 1970).

Humans have a penchant for "otherizing" as evidenced by their building of walls to separate themselves from those they consider a threat. The most famous include The Great Wall of China, the Berlin Wall, the Belfast 'Peace' Walls, and the West Bank Wall, which is sometimes referred to as the "apartheid" wall. President Donald Trump built his successful 2016 presidential campaign in large measure on the chant "Build That Wall," a reference to a barrier fantasy he espoused to gin up his followers. The Wall, he said, would keep out the Mexicans, who are "bringing drugs, they're bringing crime, they're rapists" (Mervosh, 2018).

The wall separating Palestinians from Israelis, built in the early 2000's, is perhaps the most notorious otherizing project in modern day history. While the two groups had long standing and deeply felt grievances against one another, up until the time the wall was built, there existed social, commercial, cultural, and even, at times, personal connections between them. Tens of thousands of Palestinians from the West Bank and the Gaza Strip worked in Israel. Many Israelis, in turn, shopped in the West Bank area on weekends. The two groups often attended each other's family events, some even opened businesses with one another. To be clear, there remained a lop-sided calculus of power and prestige, with the Israelis having the upper hand. However, there was, by most accounts, an apparent empathy that could only exist among those engaged in social intercourse. Until the wall. When the Oslo peace accords dissolved in 2000 and a Palestinian uprising occurred, there was a new zeitgeist in the air, one that remains today. The Israelis believed it was time for separation and built a barrier and forbade Palestinians from entering Israeli territory (Bronner, 2014).

Elaine Gross, President of ERASE Racism, an energetic advocacy group headquartered on Long Island, New York, avers that as long as people from different racial groups do not associate with one another they "inhabit very different realities." To overcome structural racism, people of different backgrounds will have to share current challenges, commit to sharing an understanding of history, and develop "empathy" for one another (Gross, 2018).[1]

My own experiences with "the other" have shaped, to a large degree, my curiosity about racial divide issues. Kristoff (2014) cites a study from the Public Religion Research Institute which suggests that in a network of 100 friends, White people have, on average, one Black friend. The ratio seems accurate to me. Over the course of my life, the personal interactions I have had with Black and Brown people have been few and far between. Below I share examples of these fraught relationships.

I have lived exclusively in White communities throughout my life. My experiences were oftentimes racially tinged and sometimes racially repugnant. Growing up, my knowledge of Black and Brown people came from stories, movies, songs, and other popular culture messaging – with one notable exception. I went to a highly regarded technical high school for one year. The student body came from all over New York City. For the first time, I was in class with students of color. I was soon disabused of my pre-conceived idea of the lassitude of "colored" people. Some of the brightest students in my classes were the Black kids. In fact, many served as role models for the lesser intellectually abled White kids. Although over 50 years ago, I can still recall the lively and interesting conversations that we had in class. Skin color seemed irrelevant.

In the next high school I attended, there were virtually no Black students. One Black girl, however, was very popular. Bright, sophisticated, and well-liked. She ran against me for vice-president of the senior class. I lost. A bunch of kids talked about me behind my back. They said that I couldn't even beat a "N-word." Rather than being appalled by the despicable reference, I was embarrassed by the suggestion.

I attended an all-White college and then taught in an all-White school district. I married a White woman and we lived in middle class White communities as we raised our children. We rarely, if ever, mingled with people of color. They were truly the "other" for my family. A glaring example of this phenomenon took place when one of my sons, who played basketball for his high school team, arrived at the gymnasium for a game with a school that was comprised mostly of kids of color. As we walked into the gym, where hundreds of black faces greeted us from the stands, I could see my son – and many of his teammates – palpably recoil as they walked to the visiting team's locker room. They simply had never been in the presence of large groups of Black people before.

Another example, one that is particularly disturbing for me personally and professionally, occurred when I was a school administrator in an all-White school district. I looked out of my office window and I saw three Black teenagers walking up the driveway of the school. I knew they could not possibly be part of our student body. I was suspicious. I watched carefully and thought about calling security. Turns out, they were on campus for legitimate reasons.

1.1   *Implicit Bias*

When driving an automobile, we call the area we cannot see at the back right corner – or left corner if we are driving in South Africa – the blind spot. Many cars are now equipped with a "blind spot indicator." If human beings came off the assembly line with the same feature, maybe we would be more able to discern biases hidden from our view.

The concept of "implicit bias" has been woven into the conversations about the racial divide. Researchers, educators, and activists have used the concept to explain how racial discrimination goes quite often unnoticed.

Over 15 million people have completed the Implicit Association Test (IAT),[2] producing a vast set of data about our implicit bias habits. As explained in *Blindspot* (Banaji & Greenwald, 2015):

> Part of what the IAT tells us when it reveals hidden biases, whether about the elderly, dark-skinned people, or gay people, is that the membrane that divides the culture "out there" from our mind "in here" is permeable. Whether we want them to or not, the attitudes of the culture at large infiltrate us … even those engaged in a fight for the rights of their stigmatized group are affected by the constant negative input from the culture …. Our minds pick up a lot of what's out there, and it seems nearly impossible to resist the pull toward culturally rooted stereotypes.

The cognitive and emotional contortions necessary to ignore the truth have handy equipment to sustain the charade. Much like the features of normalization, our minds are looking for easy answers to complex issues, answers that fit our social predilections. As the American journalist (and social critic) H. L. Mencken observed: "For every complex problem there is an answer that is clear, simple and wrong."

Schema theory suggests that when we encounter something different we look for a way to contextualize the incoming information so we can make sense of the new phenomenon. So, we tend to default to our biases about the new, incoming data. We search for (any) knowledge we already have about the subject, and use it to formulate a perspective, stance, or attitude (Haslam, 2018).

Similarly, Tversky and Kahneman (1974, as cited in Dodge, 2009) studied *heuristics*, or mental "short cuts." They investigated how and why people rely on simplified operations to explain complex phenomena. While "heuristics" as an approach to explaining things can be useful, it can also lead to "severe and systematic errors." The "availability heuristic" occurs when people assess the probability of an event by the ease with which instances or occurrences can be brought to mind." David R. Williams, a Harvard sociologist who studies the effects of implicit bias on health, states:

> As an American raised in this society with negative implicit biases against Black people, you are not a bad person. You are simply a normal American. We have to come to grips with the reality that this racism is so deeply embedded in our culture that it shapes how we see the world, it shapes our beliefs, our behavior, our actions toward members of other groups. We have to examine ourselves in a profound way. (Wilkerson, 2015)[3]

If we are prone to jump to a conclusion about something or someone without all the facts, i.e., fill in the blanks with information that may or may not be accurate, or for that matter, information that is willfully distorted, how does this ignorance affect how we engage with the world?

2   Biology Weaponized

How does skin color bias present itself in real time? What occurs when racial considerations invade policy pronouncements and political intent, decision-making, responses in social settings, the canons of research, and the everyday lives of people? Examples, both infamous and pedestrian, come to mind all too easily.

2.1   *America the Beautiful (for Some)*

Those occupying seats of power and influence often set the tone for public awareness of racial issues. Their pronouncements can provide cover for subtle malfeasance and outright license for unbridled bigotry. The United States offers a trove of hypocrisy which explodes mythology. Harvard socio-biologist Stephen Jay Gould, in his magnum opus *The Mismeasure of Man* (Gould, 1981), chronicles the unseemly musings on biological determinism of three who reside in the sacred annals of American history.

Here's Ben Franklin commenting on his preference for populating America:

> And while we are, as I may call it, scouring our planet, by clearing America of woods, and so making this side of our globe reflect a brighter light to

the eyes of inhabitants in Mars or Venus, why should we ... darken its people? Why increase the Sons of Africa, by planting them in America, where we have so fair an opportunity, by excluding all Blacks and Tawneys, of increasing the lovely White and Red? (Gould, 1981, p. 32)[4]

Thomas Jefferson had this to say about biological differences:

I advance it, therefore, as a suspicion only, that the Blacks, whether originally a distinct race, or made distinct by time and circumstance, are inferior to the Whites in the endowment both of body and of mind. (Gould, 1981, p. 32)

Abraham Lincoln, the "Great Emancipator," included this assertion in his remarks during the Lincoln/Douglas debates:

There is a physical difference between the White and Black races which I believe will forever forbid the two races living together on terms of social and political equality. And inasmuch as they cannot so live, while they do remain together there must be the position of superior and inferior, and I as much as any other man am in favor of having the superior positions assigned to the White race. (Gould, 1981, p. 35)

Furthermore, in a 1921 *Good Housekeeping* magazine essay, then vice president Calvin Coolidge wrote:

There are racial considerations too grave to be brushed aside for any sentimental reasons. Biological laws tell us that certain divergent people will not mix or blend. The Nordics propagate themselves successfully. With other races, the outcome shows deterioration on both sides. Quality of mind and body suggests that observance of ethnic law is as great a necessity to a nation as immigration law. (as cited in Ladson-Billings, 2012, p. 116)[5]

Coolidge's Nordic reference brings to mind comments made by President Donald Trump in January 2018. In an Oval Office meeting about immigration, he said, "Why are we having all these people from shithole countries come here?" referring to countries mentioned by the lawmakers who were present at the meeting. He also asked, "Why do we need more Haitians? Take them out." Trump then suggested that the United States should instead bring in more people from countries such as Norway (Dawsey, 2018).

One of the more hallowed social movements in the US was the fight for women's suffrage. Susan B. Anthony and Elizabeth Cady Stanton are towering figures in the cause to grant women the right to vote. But, there is a dark side to their story as well. In a paper, Anthony and Stanton lashed out at those supporting the passage of the 15th amendment, believing that the right to vote given to all men, regardless of race, would lead only to "degradation of women at the hands of Negro men." In 1913, as organizers of a suffragist parade in Washington prepared for the event, they demanded that Black participants march at the back of the parade instead of with their state delegations. Anthony and Stanton made the calculated decision to support one cause over the other. Although they remain heroic change agents in the annals of US politics, and are even remembered as soldiers in many abolitionist battles, the traces of racial animus remain part of their legacy (Staples, 2018).

2.2 *Exercising Caution/Deepening Distrust/Suspecting and Expecting the Worst*

Whether subliminally or consciously, we exhibit fear and enmity – and at the very least an inappropriate curiosity – of color differences in others. Being "on guard" is common. Stereotyping is par for the course. Instances illuminate the issue.

Black males were portrayed as violent, irrational, and dysfunctional in movies produced by White filmmakers in the US from the 1940s through 1960s. They have to be "physically debilitated, desexualized and medically managed" to reduce the threat they pose (Agosto, 2014).

The outsize expulsion rate for Black boys in US schools has been a topic of research for many years. Are educators' biases responsible for this? A study (by researchers at Yale University's Zigler Center) of preschool children's expulsion rates examined this question in light of a teacher's expectations. Preschool educators were asked to look for challenging behaviors, although none were actually present, in a video of preschoolers engaging in typical young child behaviors. As the educators observed the video, their eyes were tracked. Findings showed that educators gazed longer at Black children, especially Black boys (Hathaway, 2016).

Sometimes racial insinuations are found in unlikely places. While research can uncover important relationships and break new conceptual ground, a caveat is in order for those who toil in the research community. Research sources – which some might assume to be relatively immune from racial predispositions – are hardly free of biased expectations. As Gloria Ladson-Billings observes, "… racial identification underscores the way 'research' functions to serve ongoing narratives of superiority/inferiority, citizen/alien, intelligent/

unintelligent, and human/inhuman ..." (Ladson-Billings, 2012). In her inves-
tigations as a postdoctoral fellow she found that much of the literature about
African-Americans was tied to deficits and failure. As she reviewed the literature – using search terms such as "Black education" and "African American
education" – she found cross references to "see culturally deprived" and "see
culturally deficient" within two clicks! She concludes:

> Our entire field was resting on a deficit paradigm that makes it difficult to
> uncouple the work we want to do from the centuries of work handed down
> from ideological positions that emerged from constitutive disciplines
> that insist on the inferiority of entire groups of people. (Ladson-Billings,
> 2012)

In a *New York Times* piece, "Summer Road Tripping While Black," Allyson
Hobbs recounts her father's reactions when traveling with the family through
the southern United States, a region fraught with an anti-Black narrative.

> ... my father was growing more and more uncomfortable the farther south
> we drove. Once it got dark, the car fell silent .... My father later remem-
> bered that he was not anxious as we drove through Virginia, but once we
> crossed the North Carolina state line, he took a deep breath shook his
> head and sighed. "Well, we're in the South now." (Hobbs, 2018)

2.3   *In South Africa, Black Is the New White*

When I met with the faculty of one South African school – where most of the
teachers were Coloured – we discussed the current state of inequality within
their communities. I was surprised – shocked, in fact – to hear one teacher say
that in South Africa, the new face of apartheid is Black. There was unanimous
support for this position within the room. The sentiment squares with many
pundits' viewpoints and disheartening examples. (Note that the assignment
"Coloured" was distinct from "Black" in the apartheid lexicon.)

Johnson (2015) makes reference to the idea that Blacks want to play in the
luxurious game that White people got to play. He declares:

> Inevitably what Black people wanted was to be incorporated into that
> game on the basis of equality so that they too could enjoy a democratic
> political system and access or potential access to the desirable life which
> they saw Whites living. This is indeed what actually happened, so that
> very quickly there were Black millionaires, Black cabinet ministers, Black
> talk show hosts, Black professors, and so on and so forth. Black people

simply moved into the structures which they inherited from the old
White regime, most of which remained intact. (pp. 13–14)

Johnson continues his analysis of the deeply embedded characteristics in the
South African native psyche as a result of apartheid rule. He suggests that
Black people in South Africa, having lived in a police state for so long, have
internalized violent notions. As a result of inequality, they harbor resentment,
self-hate and, for the worst off, a "toxic sense of despair." One residual of apartheid rule is that Black people have learned the tactics of social denigration and
are capable themselves of racist behaviors. This is a legacy of hate, "a history
we cannot undo." He adds that many Black South Africans will not admit this
troubling manifestation. Johnson declares "… victims of racism, like victims of
sexual abuse, can become the next generation of racists and the next generation of sexual predators" (Johnson, 2015).

McKaiser (2012) shares a conundrum for Coloured people in his piece "Not
White Enough, Not Black Enough." He parses the differences in identifications
that exist as a reminder today of apartheid law. There are four racial categories: Black, Coloured, Indian and White. There are lineage iterations beyond
these four which include "bi-racial" and other "mixed" categories. During the
apartheid era, more money was spent on the Coloured community than the
Black community, but less than was spent on the White community. The racial
hierarchy was legally, politically, and economically entrenched. Today, 18 years
into democracy, many Coloured people feel that they benefit less from policies designed to redress past discrimination than Black Africans, who are seen
as worthier victims. For example, "Black Economic Empowerment" (BEE) is
designed to shift power to the Black community to redress wrongs endured
during apartheid. This leaves many Coloured people to charge: "We weren't
White enough before, and now we are not Black enough!"

That the White police force used violence against Black communities during
apartheid is common knowledge. What is a more recent development is that
police force violence is often directed at the poor, with more restraint exer-
cised in White communities which also house wealthy Black citizens who have
access to legal counsel and other resources. The police force, once an arm of
the apartheid government, is now the tool of the ANC, which is dominated by
the Black elite and the business-class White.

South Africa has been recognized on the world stage as a beacon of democracy. The truth may be quite different when corruption at the highest levels is
considered. The financing of elections is a case in point, as noted recently by a
government inquiry. A *New York Times* article, "South African Voters are Kept

in Dark on Who is Financing Campaigns" (Onishi, 2019) exposes the troubling scenario.

> Though South Africa has long been held up as a model of democratiza-
> tion, revelations at the inquiry indicate that financing of its elections
> appears to be riddled with the same kind of corrupt practices that have
> consumed the nation in recent years.

The inquiry discussed was a government investigation into corruption. One of the examples chronicled was a scheme whereby a South African company, Bosasa, would receive a request for campaign financing from the ANC and then fraudulently invoice the government for old computer software for youth centers. The company would usually end up keeping half and the other half would be paid in cash to the campaign officials.

One South African educator shared with me that, today, skin color definitions are contextualized in his country. There is a "political" Black, wherein everyone who is non-White is considered Black. And there is a socially Black, a version based on your culture as defined by the categories Black, Coloured, Indian, and White. He added that in schools, the teachers would do well to be honest about their personal frame of reference which determines in large measure how they will view the expectations they have for their students.

The new middle class in South Africa is comprised of a new Black middle class as well as the historically advantaged groups. This transmogrification of the public profile is a distortion of the course correction that Mandela and others envisioned. To wit, Subreenduth (2013) comments on the internal discourse in South Africa on education policy:

> Global, neoliberal social justice discourse on education is clearly linked
> to the global knowledge economy that prizes market efficiency, stan-
> dards, and corporate style accountability/punishment and, in South
> Africa's case, then also undermines fundamental social justice efforts of
> redress and re-humanizing the native/Black African, re-centering indig-
> enous knowledge (culture, language, ritual) as a valuable component of
> the fabric of society.

To be clear, although there exist wealthy, powerful Black people in South Africa today, *most* of the Black people are still oppressed and live in horrendous situations. I speak as an outsider who has not been subject to the influences of the internal dynamics of the South African social revolutions/evolutions. As such, perhaps it is presumptuous of me to hold a fervent viewpoint on the matter. That being said, I will share that I consider it all the more shameful that apartheid era conditions continue in South Africa despite the fact that many of the leaders/powerbrokers are Black.

2.4   *Beauty's Only Skin Deep*

In South Africa, many men and women are using skin-bleaching creams to whiten their skin in order to be more successful. An illegal industry that promotes this fashion statement capitalizes on Black citizens' desire to look "yellow bone," which is shorthand for light-skinned Black people. Use of the products, according to medical experts, can lead to skin cancer and other serious – sometimes fatal – skin diseases. (The phenomenon of lightening skin is all the more remarkable because some believe that Black skin is associated with power and wealth. The public consciousness in South Africa about variations in skin color is turbulent – and often unpredictable.)

It has been estimated that one in three men and women use dangerous skin-lightening products, most of which are illegal, across the country. One young man, a marketing student, said he has been using the products for two years and he feels more attractive now because he is "lighter." The lighter the better, he says. "I have four numbers so far," he boasts while on a night out, indicating that wouldn't be the case if he had darker skin (Brown, 2017). The potentially deadly makeover has become embedded in cultural lore. Reports of increased sexual attraction, improved chances of landing a job (celebrities claim they get more modeling work), and changes of "image" keep the product available. This, despite police raids on those who market the creams. Ironically, the chemical reaction of the creams on the skin removes the melanin that protects skin from ultraviolet sun rays which can cause skin cancer (Brown, 2017). In light of the significance that melanin content played in the early migrations of humans, it appears that the underground cosmetics industry is messing with the course of evolution.

Color envy, of course, is not restricted to South Africa. For example, West Africa has a multi-billion dollar skin whitening industry. (Ghana is flooded with "White is better" billboard ads for skin creams.) Across the ocean, Toni Morrison in an essay entitled "Mourning for Whiteness" – written after Donald Trump's election – focused on the notion in the United States that White is a superior skin color. She suggests that there are everyday assumptions associated with this feeling, including that if you are White, you will not be scrutinized in a department store (Cooper, 2016).

Then there is the photography industry in the United States. While preparing for a lecture on images and justice, Harvard professor Sarah Lewis was told by one of the technicians setting up for the video recording and lighting for the conference: "We have a problem. Your jacket is lighter than your face ... That's going to be a problem for lighting." Lewis responded to break the tension felt in the room after the technician's comment: "Well, everything is lighter than my face. I'm Black." Lewis suggests that the tech thought the problem with the lighting had to do with the degree to which her body was "unsuitable." There is an unconscious bias in photography that assumes that light skin is normal and other skin colors need "special corrective action" (Lewis, 2019).

2.5   Micro-Aggressions

Micro-aggressions might be described as subtle intrusions into the spaces occupied by the marginalized, actions which reinforce stereotypes. Most of these slights are not legally prohibited; they are a common part of everyday speech and action. "This often surprises the targets of micro-aggressions who may expect the purpose of anti-discrimination law is to prohibit this kind of harm" (Luke & Bangs, 2014, p. 3).

McKaiser (2015) points out, in South Africa, just as there existed what was once called "petty apartheid" – segregated neighborhoods, parks beaches, etc. – there exists "petty racism" today. Both are "violent assaults on the dignity of the victims," however. As an example, he says when a Black person is asked – "What are you doing walking in our suburb? You don't belong here!" – the "inherent worth of the victim is attacked" (pp. 8–9).

As a young man, Nelson Mandela and his friend Paul were walking past a post office when a White man stopped them and asked Paul to go in and buy him some stamps. (It was not uncommon in those days for a White person to ask any Black person to do a chore.) Nelson's friend refused and the White man was furious. Paul did not back down. Afterwards, Nelson felt troubled by the incident. If the man had asked him he simply would have complied. Later, he found himself admiring Paul's actions. "I was beginning to realize that a Black man did not have to accept the dozens of petty indignities directed at him each day" (Mandela, 1994, p. 50).

When I was a school administrator in a relatively wealthy community, the high school principal told me that the Black students in the school were aware of signals that White people used to warn them of potential danger. These young people, for the most part, lived in a section of the community that was originally designated as living space for the servants of the rich White people who lived in other parts of town, a phenomenon not unusual in Long Island's wealthier communities. Two signals that were common were called the "clicks" and the "buzzers." The clicks were the sound of car doors being locked as White people noticed a Black person walking near their car. The buzzers were the sounds from the public address system heard in department stores when Black teenagers walked into them, alerting store personnel.

At an educational conference, I brought up the subject of micro-aggressions – using many of the examples found here. A Black educator cautioned me about the loose use of this term by White people. While the offense may be "micro" to White people, it may be much more impactful to people of color. I offer this story as a somewhat disingenuous disclaimer in that, while I take to heart my colleague's comment, it did not deter me from writing about the subject.

2.6   *The Hottest Button*

Perhaps the most flammable of insults in the United States, one that is a standard salvo from the racist's arsenal – is the use of the term "nigger" when referring to people of color. In cleaned-up public exchanges the hate-filled calumny is tagged the "n-word." The term has deep roots in American culture, used to identify slaves and as verbal pugilism during the Jim Crow era. To this day, it is heard often in circles of unremitted bigots and those callous to the damage it wreaks. In South Africa, a parallel experience involves the word "kaffir," or the "k-word" when referenced in public. The derogation was used by European settlers and, during the apartheid regime, became the slur of choice for White people to describe native Africans. As a not unexpected postscript to the parallel, the Afrikaans term kaffir-boetie (kaffir brother) was used to describe a White person who socialized or sympathized with Black people, not far from the demonic "nigger-lover" in the states.

A brief coda for this chapter may be in order.

• • •

The emphasis in the points made is that Black and Brown people deserve equal status in society, and those attempting to undermine this right need to be challenged; skin color should not determine privilege. However, there exists a subtle irony in shining a light on this issue. Adrian Piper suggests that "the fight for liberation from oppression can reify the very same racial categories that are bogus to begin with" (Williams, 2018). In other words, by reminding us all that a problem exists around racial categorization – and refining the argument repeatedly with definitions of race – we assist in codifying the divide.

As the fight for freedom from oppression continues, an awareness of unintended consequences should be part of the work.

Notes

1 Retrieved from http://www.longislandindex.org/wp-content/uploads/2018/04/
  GROSS_essay_reprint1.pdf
  Erase Racism, under the direction of Elaine Gross, has been advocating for fair
  housing and equal educational opportunities for all Long Islanders for many years.
  Despite the intransigence of the problems, the organization has been relentless in
  its pursuit of social justice.
2 The IAT can be accessed at https://implicit.harvard.edu
3 Williams' context here is as a response to Harper Lee's, *Go Set a Watchman*, a
  follow-up story of Atticus Finch's life after the "Mockingbird" trial. In the new book,
  Lee portrays Atticus as a complex character, one who harbors racial resentments as
  well as embracing justice for all; "he is human," i.e., he is normal.
4 Gould notes that Franklin had the "decency" to include the original inhabitants in
  his vision for America.
5 Others have compared Coolidge's attitudes towards immigrants to Donald Trump's,
  most notably Dawsey (2018) in *Whose Country Is This? Trump, Coolidge and
  Immigration*.

CHAPTER 3

From Sandton to Sandtown: Tales of Two Cities

> It was the best of times, it was the worst of times, it was the age of wisdom,
> it was the age of foolishness, it was the epoch of belief, it was the epoch
> of incredulity, it was the season of Light, it was the season of Darkness,
> it was the spring of hope, it was the winter of despair, we had everything
> before us, we had nothing before us ...
>
> CHARLES DICKENS, *A Tale of Two Cities* (1859)

∵

If racism is a social scourge that divides people along ethnic and color lines, then income inequality is the sine qua non of racism. Throughout the world, wealth disparities exalt the rich and cripple the poor. In countries where the discrepancy is vast, the differences in the life experiences of those at the extremes of the continuum are almost incomprehensible. Much has been researched and written about the uneven distribution of wealth. The data reveal the dramatic gulf between rich and poor.

1   Long Division

Large-scale data which examine global wealth disparities by country can be instructive. The Organization for Economic Co-operation and Development (OECD)[1] compares countries' relative economic disparities. One measure it uses is the GINI coefficient, which represents a gauge of wealth disparity between the top 10% and the bottom 10% of the population. Recent (2019 or latest available) OECD data tables rank 38 countries from around the globe on various indicators.

Income is defined as household disposable income in a particular year. It consists of earnings, self-employment, capital income, and public cash transfers; income taxes and social security contributions paid by households are deducted. The income of the household is attributed to each of its members, with an adjustment to reflect differences in needs for households of different sizes. Of the 38 countries measured for *income inequality* in the OECD

© KONINKLIJKE BRILL NV, LEIDEN, 2020 | DOI: 10.1163/9789004444430_003

study (the 1st having the least inequality and 38th the most), South Africa has the dubious distinction of being #38, and not far behind, at #33, is the United States.

The *poverty gap* is the ratio by which the mean income of the poor falls below the poverty line. The poverty line is defined as half the median household income of the total population. The poverty gap helps refine the poverty rate by providing an indication of the poverty level in a country. On this scale, South Africa is again at the bottom at #38 and the US is #35.

The *poverty rate* is the ratio of the number of people (in a given age group) whose income falls below the poverty line, taken as half the median household income of the total population. No surprise as the pattern continues: South Africa is, once again, at the bottom and the US is #36.

1.1   *The United States*

In the United States, there exist glaring wealth disparities within the population. Wealth is the total of family assets and can provide a buffer against sudden economic downturns. The differences between the haves and the have-nots are stark and troubling.

The Urban Institute[2] has studied wealth disparity in the United States from multiple perspectives. Its findings are unsettling but not unforeseen.

Average wealth has increased over the past 50 years, but it has not grown equally for all groups.

Between 1963 and 2016

- families near the bottom of the wealth distribution (those at the 10th percentile) went from having no wealth on average to being about $1,000 in debt,
- those in the middle more than doubled their wealth,
- families near the top (at the 90th percentile) saw their wealth increase fivefold, and
- the wealth of those at the 99th percentile – in other words, those wealthier than 99 percent of all families – grew sevenfold. (Urban Institute, 2017)

When drilling down to differences along racial lines, the pattern of disparity continues.

Families of color will soon make up a majority of the population, but most continue to fall behind Whites in building wealth. In 1963, the average wealth of White families was $121,000 higher than the average wealth of non-White families. By 2016, the average wealth of White families ($919,000) was over $700,000 higher than the average wealth of Black families ($140,000) and of Hispanic families ($192,000). Put another way, White family wealth was seven times greater than Black family wealth and five times greater than Hispanic family wealth in 2016. Despite some fluctuations over the past five decades, this disparity is as high or higher than it was in 1963. (Urban Institute, 2017)

Why has wealth inequality in the US not lessened over the past 50 years and, in particular, why has the racial wealth gap not closed? The Urban Institute continued its deep dive, revealing additional insights.

Income inequality contributes to wealth inequality. Income differs from a family's assets. Both income and assets are bound together when determining a family's wealth status – and security. Having assets can provide a cushion in the wake of an economic downturn and provide a means of investment. Between 1963 and 2016, wealthy families – those at the top of the income scale – saw their income rise roughly 90% and those at the bottom of the scale, during the same period, saw their incomes rise less than 10%.

Other areas of investigation focused on the wealth gap between Whites and others.

– Differences in earnings add up over a lifetime and widen the racial and ethnic wealth gap ...
– Black and Hispanic families lag behind on major wealth-building measures, like home ownership ...
– Black and Hispanic families have less in liquid retirement savings ...
– Black families carry more student loan debt than White families ...
– Federal policies fail to promote asset building by lower-income families .... (Urban Institute, 2017)

Evidence that the gap is perpetuated by policy is apparent given that the federal government in the United States spent over $400 billion to support asset development, most of which benefited higher-income families, troubling the inequality gap even further. Lower income families may benefit from government-subsidized programs which focus on food and cash assistance, which may meet their immediate needs. Generally, however, wealth-building support for the long term, e.g., home ownership and retirement subsidies, is not available to the poor. Their plight remains fixed while those who are already comfortable become more so (Urban Institute, 2017).

1.2   *South Africa*

Any discussion of South Africa economic conditions – or social/cultural dynamics, for that matter – should include the racial breakdown of the nation. As of 2019, the Black and Coloured population accounted for almost 90% of the population while the White community accounted for just over 8%. This imbalance significantly turns up the volume on the deeply embedded inequalities uncovered in any investigation. Study after study uncovers the same grim profile; some details may vary, but the message is the same.

Chutel (2017) in a piece in *Quartz Africa* shares these dire circumstances for the Black South African community:

> One of the most enduring legacies of apartheid is the grinding poverty suffered by the country's majority Black population. Social spending on housing, healthcare, and a grant system were specifically designed to lift Black South Africans out of poverty. Black South Africans continue to be worst affected by rising poverty, with nearly half considered below Statistics South Africa's lower-bound line of poverty, defined as individuals who have to sacrifice buying food for other essentials. Less than 1% of White South Africans are below this dire line. South Africa's youth are trapped in poverty from an early age, with 43.5% of the citizens under the age of 17 living in households that earned below the median income of 797 rand ($60) per month. It's the start of a vicious cycle that continues into adulthood, with more than half of South Africans below the age of 35 unemployed. (Chutel, 2017)

The World Bank[3] has examined the situation from multiple perspectives:

> South Africa is a dual economy with one of the highest inequality rates in the world, with a consumption expenditure Gini coefficient of 0.63 in 2015. Inequality has been persistent, having increased from 0.61 in 1996. High inequality is perpetuated by a legacy of exclusion and the nature of economic growth, which is not pro-poor and does not generate sufficient jobs. Inequality in wealth is even higher: the richest 10% of the population held around 71% of net wealth in 2015, while the bottom 60% held 7% of the net wealth. Furthermore, intergenerational mobility is low, meaning inequalities are passed down from generation to generation with little change in inequality over time. Not only does South Africa lag its peers on level of inequality and poverty, it lags on the inclusiveness of consumption growth. (World Bank, 2019)

A World Bank report, *Overcoming Poverty and Inequality in South Africa: An Assessment of Drivers, Constraints and Opportunities,* examines, in part, the relationship between poverty and selected demographics.

> Poverty levels are consistently highest among femaleheaded households, Black South Africans, and children below the age of 15 and these groups tend to have a higher risk of falling into poverty .... Members of female-headed households are up to 10 percent more likely to slip into poverty and 2 percent less likely to escape poverty than members of male-headed households. Race remains a strong predictor of poverty in South Africa, with Black Africans being at the highest risk of being poor. Large families, children, and people in rural areas are especially vulnerable to being in poverty for a long time. (Sulla & Zikhali, 2018)

Other studies concur. An NPR investigate report (Beaubien, 2018), "The Country With the World's Worst Inequality Is ...," found that the vast majority of South Africans live in poverty and most of the wealth in the country is in the hands of a "small elite." The report cites a study produced by the World Bank, which found that the top 1% of South Africans own 70.9% of the wealth. The bottom 60% collectively control only 7% of the country's assets. With no equivocation, a senior economist for the World Bank, whose work covers conditions in South Africa, states: "There is no country that we have data about where the inequality is higher than in South Africa" (Beaubien, 2018).

It appears that lack of political will has been part of the seeming intractability of the problem. In 2012, the country embarked on a "National Development Plan" with much fanfare. However, it appears certain that the plan's goals, which include its aim to reduce poverty to 0% and eliminate hunger by 2030, will remain out of reach if there is not a fundamental change of course.

1.3   *This Can't Be True*

The data uncovered through an examination of the two countries in this study offer a lens through which we can see an unfair, even unconscionable, wealth gap. A look at the numbers gleaned from *worldwide* wealth disparity puts more local findings in perspective. The global macro data related to the mega-rich and abject-poor are the stuff of fiction – where exaggeration is expected.

According to Forbes,[4] in 2014, the 85 richest people in the world had as much money as the 3.5 billion poorest. Hard as it is to believe, things got more extreme in the following four years. OXFAM,[5] in 2019, reports that in 2018, the 26 richest people had as much money as the 3.8 billion poorest. The report continues: the wealth of the billionaire class increased by $900 billion dollars a year ($2.5 billion a day) while the poorest half of the world's wealth declined by 11%. In the US, the 30 richest people had as much money as the poorest half of the population.

And, to put a familiar face on the disparity, Jeff Bezos, owner of Amazon, was reputed to be worth $170 billion dollars in 2018, making him the richest man in the world. Bezos's personal fortune was greater than the individual GDPs (the gross domestic product/the total value of everything produced in a country) of 133 countries (according to the International Monetary Fund list of 190 countries).[6]

2   The Effects Downstream

David Berliner, channeling the wisdom of Desmond Tutu,[7] tells the story of two doctors who are walking by a stream. Suddenly, they hear a shout from the water. A man is struggling for his life as the stream is carrying him away. The doctors, both good Samaritans, make their way into the stream and revive the man. They walk a bit further and see another individual crying out for help, another victim of the stream's force. After reviving this person, they move on and, lo and behold, another one needs help. After this episode, one of the doctors begins rushing ahead of his companion who asks where he's going. The other replies: "I'm going upstream to find out why they're falling in."

Global comparisons of wealth disparity and the concomitant impacts on social well-being and basic competencies, beg the question: What does this disparity look like on the ground? How does the worldwide economic schism manifest when drilled down to localities, the smaller divisions of the social landscape? Cities and towns and municipalities throughout the world are wildly uneven in wealth and therefore equally uneven in providing services to their populations.

Examples are all too readily available.

2.1   *Sandton and Alexandra ...: A Kilometer (and a World) Apart*
On my first trip to South Africa, our group visited the city of Sandton, near Johannesburg proper. It is a magnificent place, a reminder of the most upscale residential and commercial areas in the United States. The group then passed by the township of Alexandra. The differences were startling. The landscape changed from extraordinary luxury to crushing poverty in the blink of an eye. The experience prompted me to write a letter to Nelson Mandela in my journal, one that I never sent, but am happy to share now. (Madiba was Mandela's tribal name.)

Dear Madiba,   *March 2008*

I just returned from a trip to your beautiful country. My excursions included meetings with South African educators and students, sight-seeing and a safari at the wondrous Kruger National Park. My adventure was nothing short of brilliant.

With one exception.

It will come as no surprise to you that the gaping disparity between the haves and have nots in South Africa is evident wherever you travel. A prime example that my group experienced was when we journeyed to Stellenbosch, a town reminiscent of the Hamptons, an exclusive area in my home state in the US. Then, just 20 minutes away, we drove past a township of utter despair and abject poverty. The "homes" were no more than 8 by 8 corrugated metal, boxed together by the hundreds – or maybe the thousands.

In my naivete about your country, I assumed that 15 years after apartheid we would not see this unspeakable poverty amidst luxury. I know you are in your democratic infancy and I have nothing but optimism because your people are so resilient.

But all of this you know. I don't write to remind you that there is work to be done. But there is something that you are, perhaps, not aware of, and it has more to do with the symbolic aspect of change. I ask you to consider the following.

I visited Mandela Square in Sandton. It was a magnificent mall of shops, restaurants, and boutiques. In the square there is a 50-foot statue of you, that is impressive and inspiring. When I visited, at the foot of the statue there was an Aston Martin sales exhibition. One of the most expensive cars in the world was being sold at the feet of the nation's liberator and a world paragon of social justice. The dissonance at the moment I saw this was over-whelming. I could not help but have images of township horrors in sharp counterpoint to an Aston Martin automobile.

I know my own country has much work to do regarding economic dispar-ities. The housing projects of our inner cities juxtaposed against the afflu-ence of our suburbs is just one glaring example. Maybe it is because I was looking to South Africa to have done better that I am disappointed that it has not.

So, Madiba, I hope you will not mind my impertinence when I ask you to consider sharing with your countrymen that an outsider's view of South Africa should not be tainted by images of luxury items – items which only the few have access to, so close to a symbol of freedom – a right which all are entitled to.

Sincerely,

A traveler in your beloved country

Sandton is regarded by many as one of the most important business districts in all of Africa with some of the most impressive shopping venues in the world. (See the depiction in the next paragraph.) It also contains rows of stately homes in manicured neighborhoods. (I had the opportunity to drive through these communities and get a look, firsthand, at the opulence.) Interesting to note that this residential and commercial profile has remained the same for over 50 years and the Sandton Mall was built 30 years ago. The end of apartheid notwithstanding, these markers of the rich remain intact today.

The information below comes from the ABOUT US section of one of the Sandton City Mall websites.

> Imagine a place where the likes of Hugo Boss and Louis Vuitton, Carrol Boyes and Apple showcase their very best ranges; a place where you can sip on the world's finest coffee or enjoy a French croissant or a slice of local milk tart – all under one roof.
>
> If you can imagine it, then you've pictured Sandton City, one of Africa's leading and most prestigious shopping centres. Sandton City offers an unparalleled shopping experience that combines the world's most desirable brands with everyday leisure and entertainment.
>
> Situated in the prestigious Sandton Central Management District in northern Johannesburg, Sandton City is conveniently located within walking distance of the Sandton Gautrain station and within easy access from highways and main roads within Sandton CBD.
>
> With more than 300 leading local and international retailers, Sandton City is a one-of-a-kind premier fashion and leisure destination. It's an energetic hub of Afro-cosmopolitan glamour – international shopping with South African flair.[8]

In addition to the shopping center, Sandton is home to the Johannesburg Stock Exchange, the Sandton Convention Center, and ... a polo club.

Right next door – just across the M1 highway – is Alexandra, once home to Nelson Mandela. The area is virtually treeless and is laid out in a grid, a product of apartheid-era urban planning. The original area was designed for about 70,000 people; the current population is estimated to be anywhere from 180,000 to 750,000. The overcrowding, which is in large measure due to "back-yard shacks" – spaces rented in the backyard of homes – makes it virtually impossible to service the township infrastructure systems.

The first time I passed Alexandra on the highway, I was not sure what it was. The driver told me that it was a dangerous area and I should not attempt to go into it: "You won't come out alive." At the time, I was on my way to a hotel – which was a 10-minute drive from the township. The hotel was stunning and showcased a Las Vegas-style casino. (The hotel complex was not located in Sandton. It was, however, another reminder of just how close unbridled wealth is from unmitigated poverty in the country.)

I did venture into Alexandra to visit a school on one of my trips. The driver and I traveled through the streets and made our way to the barbed-wire fences of a primary school. Once inside, I spent time touring the building – and the grounds – with the principal who was overwhelmed with issues related to the students in her charge. She told me that the school was overcrowded – almost 1,200 learners in a school built for 800. One class had 60 students in it. We walked in and I was introduced to the class. I was once again reminded that, despite deplorable conditions, the South African youngsters are warm, friendly, engaging, courteous, very smart – and curious, wanting to know a lot about me.

2.2 Sandtown and Clarksville: Same State, Different Realities
Side-by-side and close-by living arrangement discrepancies between the wealthy and the poor are all too common in the United States. Throughout the country, upscale homes and private manors are found within the same vicinity as dilapidated and dangerous living quarters. This is the case in many locations in the New York region, especially the suburb of Long Island. This area is regarded as one of the most segregated regions in the United States. There are typically well-known demarcations, e.g., highways and train tracks, so that the wealthy are aware of the dangers on one side and the poor know there is "no trespassing" onto the other side. Most states around the country have similar divides and the unspoken (unspoken at least in public forums) rules of engagement.

Clarksville, Maryland, is a community approximately 24 miles north of Washington D.C., and 20 miles southwest of Baltimore. Clarksville is located in Howard County, the second wealthiest county in the United States and the location of some of the most expensive homes on the East Coast. The schools in Howard County are among the highest ranked in the country and are funded at significantly higher rates than other schools in the area.

A look at the real estate profile in Clarksville – as of 2019 – is illuminating. One real estate website offers this information to the prospective home buyer: "There are 36 homes for sale, ranging from $375,000 to $2,775,000. The median Listing Home Price is $825,000." One single family home is advertised as follows: "Price $1,275,00, $6,303 per month (est.) 6 bedrooms 5 baths 8,594 sq ft."[9]

Another real estate website issues a glowing – almost poetic – description of the area:

> Home to the Clarksville Environmental Area, the community is filled with gorgeous nature trails packed full of plants and wildlife. Because of the town's tranquil scenery and its desirable geographic location, Clarksville real estate is a very hot commodity. Homes for sale in Clarksville, Maryland, are often large single-family home units, although other residential units, such as apartments, can also be found. Generally, most of the available real estate lies close to the area's shopping centers and fine dining establishments. Because there is a booming economy in Clarksville, commercial real estate property is also popular.[10]

And this from the Howard County website:

> The County is continually ranked among the most affluent, advanced and educated communities in the United States. There is immediate access to leading educational and health care institutions, upscale retail, and outstanding recreation and entertainment. It is currently home to 110,370 households and boasts a thriving, vibrant economy and welcoming business environment, with proximity to 50 federal agencies, universities, Fortune 500 companies, technology, defense and health care companies.[11]

Northeast of Howard County is Baltimore County. They share a border. Within Baltimore County, lies Baltimore City and Sandtown-Winchester. Both areas have the dubious distinction of capturing the national spotlight for civil unrest. Sandtown-Winchester has been a particular target of criticism. (In the summer of 2019, President Donald Trump described Baltimore as a "rat and rodent infested mess" where "no human being would want to live" and "far worse and more dangerous" than the conditions at the southern border (Kimball, 2019).)

The Baltimore riot of 1968, which lasted from April 6 to April 14, and whose immediate cause was the assassination of Dr. Martin Luther King on April

4, marked a watershed moment for the city. Crowds looted and burned local businesses and had violent confrontations with the police – and the national guard. It was a moment of disturbing, public, real-life drama that reverberated around the country.

After the riots, the city remained under siege from within. Closed businesses did not reopen, residents fled the area, violence and drug use became rampant. Sandtown may have been hit the hardest. The population saw a dramatic decline and disrepair continued into the 1970s. By 2015, a third of the houses were abandoned and one fifth of the residents were unemployed. Nearly a third of families lived below the poverty line. In that year, Sandtown was again victimized, this time by an incident that left a notorious and indelible stain on its reputation and created further misery for the hardscrabble life of its citizens.

On April 12, 2015, the Baltimore Police Department in the neighborhood of Sandtown-Winchester, arrested Freddie Gray, a 25-year-old Black man. Gray sustained serious injuries to his spine while being delivered to the police station in a police vehicle. He lapsed into a coma and died one week later. Protests were organized by local citizens who believed that the police were not forthcoming about the details of Gray's death. Some protests turned violent. At least 250 people were arrested and at least twenty police officers were injured. The city declared a state of emergency and Maryland National Guard troops were called up. Gray's death was ruled a homicide and six officers were charged with various offenses, including second-degree murder. Three of the officers were acquitted and charges were dropped for the other three.

The Freddie Gray incident became seared into the nation's consciousness. Other incidents only increased the tension between police and African-Americans. Set in a neighborhood rife with violence and extreme poverty, Freddie Gray's death echoed the ghastly narrative too often heard in the United States' inner city.

Baltimore Mayor Catherine Pugh was accompanied by journalists in a 2018 tour of the Sandtown area. The article described the depressing profile of the neighborhood three years after the Freddie Gray incident.

> ... residents carry on in a landscape pockmarked with the signs of continuing decay and neglect. Over the summer, a rash of fires broke out in the vacant rowhouses here. On Winchester Street, one of those vacants collapsed two months ago and was demolished, leaving behind a crater-like depression – the building's former basement. Since then, residents complain, "The Hole" has become a trash-filled haven for addicts and drug traffickers. Webb [a police department official] pointed

out the decrepitude of the block's vacants, how one house was "snapping and bowing out," how "just yesterday we were watching them where they're running into the alleys and using the vacants for their narcotics. (Shen, 2018)

The stark differences in living conditions between many cities and regions in the same country are the result of designs drawn up and made to last by the wealthy and the powerful. This calculus impacts services to children, the most vulnerable of its victims.

2.3   *Suffer the Little Children*

I am thankful to the Nobel committee for recognizing the plight of millions of children who are suffering in this modern age. (Kailash Satyarthi, Indian Children's Rights Activist/Nobel Peace Prize winner 2014)

Throughout my years championing for civil rights, analyzing politics and advocating on behalf of the voiceless, I am disturbed the most when harmless children suffer because of politics or detrimental policies. (Al Sharpton, activist and media host)

Nic Spaull (2015), a professor at the University of Stellenbosch and a researcher and writer who addresses the economic and social conditions in South Africa, takes on the education divide based on parent wealth.

While the rich get education, SA's poor just get 'schooling.' The tragic reality in South Africa is that if your parents are in the 'top' part of the labour market (the 15%) then you send your children to the 'top' part of the schooling system (which charges fees). That gives your children access to university and to that same 'top' part of the labour market that you are currently in. If you are in the 'bottom' part of the labour-market (the 85%) then the only schools that you can afford and that are available are the second-tier no-fee schools. However, these schools are of an extremely low quality and the only way to get access to university is in spite of them.

Another moment in my visit to the Alexandra school had on it the violent signature often visible within the community and schools. After my tour of the school, when it was time for me to leave, the principal looked out of her office window and told me that I should not leave yet. She said there were young men outside the gate "waiting for you." They had seen a "White man" walk in and thought I would be an easy target for robbery on the way out. The principal called the police and we were escorted out of the township. This was one of the most distressing moments in all of my visits. In my conversations with her, the principal said this: "Poverty is the problem which leads to violence. Kids drop out of school in 7th grade and then have nothing to do and they get involved in crime, drugs, etc." I should add that during the taxi ride out of the township I observed some of the most deplorable living conditions I had ever seen in South Africa.

The United States provides stark proof, as well, of how the divide impacts youngsters. Examples of the gap between the haves and have-nots – and its effect on children – can exist within the very same city, on the very same street. A news piece entitled "The Tale of Two New York Cities" (Schuster, 2016) provides the details.

On 26th Street and 10th Avenue in West Chelsea, Manhattan, two sides of the same street demonstrate differences that are stark. On one side is Avenues, an elite private school costing $50,000 a year in tuition. The children of celebrities and tech millionaires attend. Just across the street is the Chelsea-Elliot public housing project, where thousands of people reside, many living below the poverty line.

Rosa, a 10-year-old living in the projects, shares a disturbing perspective on her life:

> The best part of growing up in the projects is that you learn how to live as a poor child. The bad thing is, you suffer a lot and you see a lot of things you're not supposed to see at this age. Like the shootouts and all that stuff. We lost a good friend of ours a long time ago, Dante. It was really sad. Thank God I'm on the 20th floor, so I don't see it, only hear it. But I feel safe. My mom has been living there for 25 years with my three brothers. Our family doesn't do trouble. Ain't nobody going to touch me.

Isabella, age 17, a twelfth grader at Avenues, made this comment about the profile of her classmates:

> Everyone at Avenues is pretty well-off, but there are some people who wear that on their sleeve and brag about wearing designer clothes, and how they take private cars to school every day, and their apartments, and their houses in the Hamptons. There are other people who are more

humble. When you go to Avenues, if you're upper-middle class you can seem poor to some people, so it skews your perspective a bit.

2.4   *More of the S(h)ame*

To capture the most understandable messages for the reader, I have attempted to organize the points made around themes and – to the extent possible – with references to both South Africa and the United States. Below, I depart from this approach to share select observations and facts which I believe need to be part of the conversation.

As I visit schools in the New York region, I am struck by the disparate circumstances from one town to the next. In a particularly stark example, there are towns on Long Island that are notoriously uneven in resources. I was standing on a street which connects two such towns with my colleague from South Africa, who was visiting. We turned to one side and looked down the street. There, a few blocks from where we were standing were tree-lined streets with magnificent homes surrounded by manicured gardens. The street where we were standing was filled with two story buildings on both sides. The first floor housed stores and the second apartments. We turned to each other and agreed: Looks a bit like South Africa. Incidentally, the schools in these two towns are often highlighted for their gross differences.

According to one estimate from a South African principal there is one nurse and one social worker for 51 schools in his region of the country.

The quintile system in South Africa divides schools into five categories, wherein quintile one schools are designated "no fee" schools and receive the largest government subsidy, up through quintile five schools which receive the smallest subsidy. A school's designation is based on relative income, unemployment and illiteracy in its geographic area. In October 2014, we stopped at a school in Paarl, South Africa – a quintile five school – and took photos and toured the buildings. We saw the magnificent grounds and talked with two White boys. They said there was a small percentage of Black students enrolled in the school. They added that these students had to be good at sports to get in to the school. The campus was jaw-droppingly beautiful. Swimming pool, trophy case, magnificent grounds including professional-sized athletic fields, etc.

On one of my trips, I visited Kayamandi, a township not far Stellenbosch. (Stellenbosch is a fabulously wealthy community where the University of Stellenbosch is located.) I got out of the car, while in Kayamandi, to talk with a woman who had just come out of a house. She told me that she does not have running water and she just comes to this house to use the bathroom. A store-owner in Stellenbosch told me that life in Kayamandi is awful: violence (even beheadings of children!), corruption, theft, etc., are every day realities. There are streets in Kayamandi that he will not walk down for fear of losing his life. He also told me that when he goes home he has to go with a cab driver who has a gun, since many in his community know that he has cash from his business with him.

As you drive down certain streets or highways in South Africa you come across premier car dealerships – Jaguar, Land Rovers, BMW, etc. Many have installed awnings to protect the cars from the elements. This sight imposes itself on the observer, in many cases, soon after traveling through a township. The juxtaposition is maddening.

Notes

1   The OECD (http://www.oecd.org/) is an international organization comprised of democratic, free-market-economy countries. The consortium works with member nations to address challenges in economic and social policy areas, including education.

2   The Urban Institute (https://www.urban.org) is a nonprofit research group which focuses on people and places in the United States to improve public policy and strengthen communities.

3   The World Bank (www.worldbank.org) has 189 member countries partnering in a global initiative to create sustainable solutions to poverty and build prosperity in developing countries.

4   Forbes (www.forbes.com) is a global media company which focuses on issues related to business, technology, leadership, lifestyle, etc.

5   Oxfam (www.oxfam.org) is a global organization working to end poverty and address issues related to food, water, farming, disaster response, climate change, and social justice

6   See tables on the International Monetary Fund website (https://www.imf.org/en/search#q=GDP&sort=relevancy).

7   Tutu's original quote was: "There comes a point where we need to stop just pulling people out of the river. We need to go upstream and find out why they're falling in." Berliner's story was told at an educators' conference on the effects of poverty.

8   See https://nelsonmandelasquare.co.za/sandton-city/

9   See https://www.zillow.com/homedetails/7233-Preservation-Ct-Fulton-MD-20759/58256602_zpid/

10 See https://www.longandfoster.com/MD/Clarksville

11 See https://www.howardcountymd.gov/About-HoCo

CHAPTER 4

The Invisible Man

> I am an invisible man. I am a man of substance, of flesh and bone, fiber
> and liquids – and I might even be said to possess a mind. I am invisible,
> understand, simply because people refuse to see me.
>
> RALPH ELLISON, *The Invisible Man* (1952)

∴

Ellison's quote kick starts a conversation about our inability to "see" one another. A simple fable about perception animates the point.

A traveler from America – where everyone wears yellow sunglasses – visits Japan. While there he notices that all the people are wearing blue sunglasses. He decides to put on the blue glasses to better understand the Japanese culture. After a two month stay, he determines that he has learned about the values and beliefs and habits of the people. He concludes that the culture of Japan is "green." Turns out, he forgot to remove his own yellow sunglasses (Mercil, 2009).

The moral of the fable presents us with a challenge. Before we can be open to other cultures – and truly "see" what they are like – we have to remove our own filters so we can notice and appreciate the differences. How do we remove a lifetime of experiencing the world through our own "sunglass" filters? We can start with a true examination of our own values, attitudes, and beliefs. The more we come to understand – and articulate – who we are, the more likely it is that we can understand others. First comes a recognition that we are actually wearing a lens which colors our world. Then, perhaps, other cultures' colors will begin to become more visible.

West (2005) contextualizes the problem as a power issue.

> The modern Black diaspora problematic of invisibility and namelessness
> can be understood as the condition of relative lack of power for Blacks to
> present themselves and others as complex human begins, and thereby
> to contest bombardment of negative, degrading stereotypes put forward
> by White supremacist ideologies (p. 35).

© KONINKLIJKE BRILL NV, LEIDEN, 2020 | DOI: 10.1163/9789004444430_004

1   **Color Blindness – A Disorder of the Privileged**

> We do not see things as they are. We see things as we are. (Rabbi Shemuel ben Nachmani, Talmudic Scholar)

In a powerful missive on the invisibility of people of color – *Colorblind Approaches to Education are Hurting Students* – French and Simmons (2015) assert: "When educators say, 'I'm colorblind' and claim not to see or be influenced by their students' race, the net result is that students of color, their experiences, and their perspectives become 'invisible' in the classroom" (p. 21). This conclusion, a result of research conducted in the Boston Public Schools, is echoed by others who have examined the mysteries of "color blindness."

White people enjoy baked-in promises from White society that they will be recognized as legitimate participants in social settings. Ruth Anne Olson (1992), building on the work of Peggy McIntosh (1988),[1] ticks off the various privileges she and her family have in public school settings as White people. For example:

- whatever her children study, they can be confident that they will find people of their race linked to historical accomplishments and faces like theirs will be liberally represented in school textbooks, etc.;
- the color of her children's skin prompts a neutral or positive assumption when they enter school offices;
- her children are confident that they will never be embarrassed by teachers asking them to share stories about their race or culture;
- when she visits school, she knows that staff will reserve judgement about her economic class, level of education and her reason for being in the school.

(Of particular note is the fact this list was written nearly 30 years ago, but remains relevant today.)

The calculated systems for keeping certain people apart from others perpetuate the social dynamics. Wells (2009) suggests that the boundaries we set up for living arrangements are the single most important determinant of the disparate opportunities for school children. "The fact that these disparities are so starkly defined by race/ethnicity and social class should give us pause in a country that likes to think of itself as 'post-racial' and 'colorblind'" (Wells, 2009).

McKaiser (2012) refers to the controversies associated with the categorization of South African citizens post-apartheid. Should the categories continue to be part of the public conversation? Or, should they be forsworn as a remnant of a past rife with racism? McKaiser's answer is provocative.

This nimble racial footwork, which often baffles outsiders, is the noxious result of racism's history. It is also the kind of result that has some people think all race talk is undesirable. I disagree. I think the language of race is honest because it captures how many of us here experience racial identities in South Africa post democracy, in terms of skewed access to economic justice .... Rather than mandate nonracial identities, we must eliminate racism. Colorblindness is the wrong antidote. (McKaiser, 2012)

Style (1996) sees the school curriculum as both a window and a mirror, contending that,

... students' educational diet is not balanced if they see themselves in the mirror all of the time. Likewise, democracy's school curriculum is unbalanced if a Black student sits in school, year after year, forced to look through the window upon the (validated) experiences of White others while seldom, if ever, having the central mirror held up to the particularities of her or his own experience. Such racial imbalance is harmful as well to White students whose seeing of humanity's different realities is also profoundly obscured. (p. 38)

Michelle Alexander (2010), in her magnum opus, *The New Jim Crow/Mass Incarceration in the Age of Colorblindness*, tackles the issue head on. In an interview she suggests:

The mythology of colorblindness takes the race question off the table. It makes it difficult for people to even formulate the question: Could this be about something more than individual choices? Maybe there is something going on that's linked to the history of race in our country and the way race is reproducing itself in modern times .... It makes it difficult to see that the backlash against the Civil Rights Movement manifested itself in the form of mass incarceration, in the form of defunding and devaluing schools serving kids of color. (as cited in Sokolower, 2011, p. 15)

In a review of Mark Warren's (2010) *Fire in the Heart, How White Activists Embrace Racial Issues*, in which he interviewed 50 White people who are involved in activist arenas, Albrecht (2012) refers to salient points made by the author.

We don't have many opportunities to interact cross-racially; thus, few White people have meaningful relationships with people of color .... Without meaningful relationships, we fall back on racist media stereotypes of people of color, and using what we think is well-intentioned language we say we are "color-blind." This insidious form of racism implies that we don't see color when we look at someone .... Unless you are a person without sight, all of us see race. (Albrecht, 2012)

French and Simmons (2015), authors of research discussed earlier, ask us to have an honest conversation about race:

Many well-intentioned teachers use this colorblind approach, but it is the wrong response for Black and Latino boys, who may experience daily instances of prejudice and racism. Research suggests that using curriculum and instruction that is explicit about race and the impact of racism in schools and society promotes school cultures in which students of color feel more of a sense of belonging and empowerment. Such school cultures can lead to better outcomes for students of color. A colorblind approach flies in the face of that knowledge. When educators say, 'I'm colorblind' and claim not to see or be influenced by their students' race, the net result is that students of color, their experiences, and their perspectives become 'invisible' in the classroom. (pp. 19, 21)

Can privileged White people fathom the concept of people of color feeling invisible? After all, we are used to thinking of those folks as victimized by people who recognize and expose the difference. But, the other offense, perhaps more insidious, is to ignore the difference and treat it as a vestige of things gone by. Maybe it takes a person of color to share experiences that expose the hurt. This is something poet Morgan Parker (2019) herewith delivers in a sardonic message about life in school for a Black student:

I have a body. It sits in a
desk.
Every day is bitten with
new guilt.
My teacher can see right
through me, all the way
to Black History Month

1.1   *Intent v. Impact*
Questioning the intent behind something a person says or does that may be regarded as hurtful, is a garden variety, everyday life experience for most of us. We may be confronted by the offended party and quickly explain that we

didn't mean anything by it. The matter can get complicated when the actors in the exchange are of a different color. A quandary arises when people of good faith, who believe that they care for everyone equally – and therefore profess they are colorblind – ignore the perspective that people of color are regularly diminished in society. They may be oblivious to the impact of words or deeds that they consider harmless, but in fact are hurtful and damaging to others.

White people are often dismayed that they might be considered contributors to racism. Gorski (2010) suggests these folks are inured to the continuing trials of people of color as they insist: "I'm not burning any crosses. I don't own slaves. (And neither did my great-grandparents!) So this racism thing isn't my issue, right." Gorski (2010) responds to this line of thinking: "As long as I can understand racism as individual acts of wacko White people, I can pretend that I have no part in it."

The annals of United States jurisprudence are rife with attempts to close down opportunities for minorities. In an unapologetic and full-throated rationale for bigotry in the US, the Supreme Court in *Mobile v. Bolden* (1980) ruled on a case involving minority representation in Mobile, Alabama. Stipulating that the situation was what the plaintiffs claimed – that it was virtually impossible for Black voters to gain representation in a city commission – the court, nevertheless, found for the defendant. The rationale was that there was no "proof of intent" shown, i.e., the city never "intended" to shut out Black people from the vote. This new standard set an impossibly high bar for others who sought redress for voter suppression (Rutenberg, 2015). (While the impact of the Mobile decision was blunted by renewals of the Voting Rights Act, the disenfranchisement of minorities remains a major point of contention in the public conversation in the US.)

In his call for a reckoning for White people in the face of the abuses of power and privilege, Mindell (1995) suggests:

> You can't apologize for racism while you are contributing to it .... Your present situation in life – the job you have, the place you live and the opportunities you have in this society – are based on the attitude the Western world takes toward People of Color. History is not just in the past. It creates the present. (p. 148)

He weighs in on the ranking, "like money in the bank," that exists by dint of color differences.

> Even if you are the least successful White person around, public feeling toward you in this country will almost always be more positive than

toward a Person of Color. Furthermore, you have a choice. You have the privilege of not dealing with prejudice because of your color. You can ignore bigotry whenever you feel like it, but a Black person must face it every day." (Mindell, 1995, p. 148)

Mindell's comments are not only instructive, but his choice of emphasis also adds to the discussion. Why does he choose to capitalize so many of his references to color? What is appropriate in this decision? While it may seem trite to some, it may also seem important to others. I am confused about this issue, as I am about many others related to a sensitive – and sensible – approach to my initiatives, interactions, and deportment regarding racially-themed social intercourse.

With regard to my own writing, should I use White or white? Do I write White privilege or white privilege? Should I be consistent? i.e., if I capitalize Black, should I also capitalize White? In speaking, do I say colored people or people of color? Should I always say Black and Brown people instead of simply Black people? These largely academic questions raise the specter of a well-known volatile challenge, one referred to earlier, in Chapter 2.

Why does the "n-word" – and the "k-word" – deliver such power? If we feel compelled not to use these words in our speech – and sometimes downright frightened if we do – are we purposely walking tiptoe around the issue by way of our politeness or fear? Is our intent not to offend or is it to protect ourselves from harm? What is the impact if we are not sincere in our choice to clean up our language? The questions raise other personal considerations for my work with regard to intent and impact.

I thought I would offer a unique experience to those who accompanied me on my South Africa sojourns. I was going to offer a RA – "Racists Anonymous" – session for all. I pursued the idea, believing that the group's thick skin would be more important than their Black or White skin in opening up about their own racist tendencies. The protocol for the meeting would be for the leader – that would be me – to begin the session with "Hi, my name is Arnie and I'm a racist." I would then share with the group the pain I inflicted on others – both knowingly and inadvertently. And, how I was happy to be in recovery.

I floated the idea with some of the folks in our group. The reaction from a few of the Black travelers was strong and definite. One said that I simply did not know the power of the word "racist" to a Black person. The very thought of going through the exercise of White people sharing their racist remarks, actions, etc. was repugnant. It would feel as though they were just props for the White folks to have an intellectual exercise, their own dignity as participants ignored. I was so very glad that I had that feedback and realized that for some in the audience the impact of the experience would have been harmful, although my intent was innocent.

And one more mea culpa for the record: I am confused regarding recognizing people of color in my classes. (Because of the settings where I have taught, most of my students have been White.) Do I ignore the difference or do I openly engage the class in a discussion about the backgrounds of the few students of color?

I "exposed" a Black boy in my ninth grade English class, while we were talking about the play, *A Raisin in the Sun*. I asked him what he thought about the themes of prejudice in the book since he was a Black boy and would probably be able to help us understand the problem. He was mortified. He self-consciously laughed and didn't say much of anything. I felt foolish. Many other times, when I had only 1 to 2 Black students in my classes, I was hesitant and confused about what to say to them when issues of race came up. Even to this day, in my graduate classes, I am uncertain. Do I say something – or not? While my intent may be innocent, I struggle with the impact.

In one of the most important inflection points in US educational history in relation to race issues, *Brown v. Board of Education* marked an historic victory for desegregation advocates. However, while the intent of the achievement was laudable, the impact may have long-term deleterious effects, an opinion proffered by Derrick Bell. Bell wrote a scathing indictment of the putatively beneficent desegregation for many African American children, even taking on the twentieth century's most iconic representation of the White community's largesse, *Brown v. BOE*. Lynn et al. (2010) unpack Bell's perspective:

> This is a counter narrative that begins with the notion of African American children having simply vanished on the "implementation day for the new desegregation plan" (Bell, 1992, p. 102). He does not explain how they vanished or where they went. He explains the impact of this legislation on Black schools: They were closed, and Black teachers and principals were fired. He noted that it was Whites, not Blacks, who stood to gain the most from the losses experienced by African American children, who would become "invisible" or lost in all-White schools where they were not wanted or appreciated ... these students were ultimately framed as oppositional. In this sense, Bell is using the parable to argue that *Brown v. Board of Education* did not significantly improve the lives of African American children. Instead, it made them even more invisible. (Lynn et al., 2010, p. 2)

In a series of studies, Rutgers University psychologist Kent Harber examined White middle school and high school teachers in mostly White, upper-middle-class districts and more diverse, working-class districts in the northeastern United States. He found that when White teachers give feedback on a poorly written essay, they are more critical if they think the author was a White student rather than a Black one. In their attempts to be egalitarian, they might avoid constructive criticism that would benefit Black students. Giving feedback is difficult for teachers in any circumstance, Harber points out. Teachers must strike a balance between being assertive and respectful. "Add the issue of race and teachers might worry they're displaying a lack of racial sensitivity. That can tip the scale and lead to a positive bias" (Weir, 2016, p. 45).[2]

Author Christopher Emdin says of growing up in public schools – as an African American child –one had to "... learn to suppress who you are, but more dangerous than suppression, you learn to devalue the things that make you ...." He continues:

> One big problem ... is the dominant narrative in public education about do-gooder teachers working to save poor kids from their troubled communities. It's a narrative that teaches young people that they hail from worthlessness, and that in order to make it in life they need to leave their homes and themselves behind. Students quickly receive the message that they can only be smart when they are not who they are .... (Brown, 2016)

1.2   *Artistic Worthiness in the Hands of White Folks*

The fabric of the arts – and the priorities regarding the worthiness of cultural meaning-making – is woven with threads chosen by the powerful. The messages therein are reflective of the norms and representations of the ruling class. The marginalized contribute to the mix, but only after the endorsement of the majority. They, by and large, do not participate in the production of the creative artifacts of the group, or if they do participate, their work is subject to the imprimatur of those with power.

Cornel West (2005) shares his views on the subject.

> The existential challenge to the new cultural politics of difference can be stated simply: How does one acquire the resource to survive and the cultural capital to thrive as an artist and a critic? ... I mean not only the high-quality skills required to engage in cultural practices, but more importantly, the self-confidence, discipline, and perseverance necessary for success without an undue reliance on the mainstream for approval and acceptance .... The widespread modern European denial

of the intelligence, ability, beauty, and character of people of color puts a tremendous burden on critics and artists of color to 'prove' themselves in light of norms and models set by White elites whose own heritage devalued and dehumanized them. (p. 38)

In relation to cultural dissemination, Berry and Yang (2019) take on the dominance of the White male critic in the art world. Their claim is that in major media outlets, White critics set the parameters for the conversation. They examined reviews of the Whitney Biennial held in New York City, an event showcasing mostly artists of color and considered by many the country's "preeminent art show." Although there were some reviewers of color, their critiques were much less visible than the White reviewers' critiques, a "dynamic shaped by the perception that the opinions of people of color are niche." Yang and Berry wax philosophical about the importance of perspective in cultural critiques. "Reviews create momentum that shape economic and intellectual marketplaces." They continue: "Think of cultural criticism as civic infrastructure that needs to be valued, not based just on its monetary impact but, also on its capacity to expand the collective conversation at a time when it is dangerously contracting" (Berry & Yang, 2019, p. 10).

And, the usurpation of worthiness of cultural opinion writing takes on an added insult in the story of a Nigerian woman who lives and works in her home country and has a strong reputation as a writer. She says that her books still have to pass muster with "White people" if they are to be well-received. The West makes decisions of cultural competency even on the African continent (Nwaubani, 2014).

2   "Linguistic Genocide"

In order to be "visible" in the world, an individual's cultural expression has to be recognized and valued. This prerequisite holds true for linguistic expressions, the medium we use to navigate in social traffic. An individual's language identity is an individual's imprint on the world.

In a presidential address given at the 2015 American Education Research Association (AERA) convention in Chicago, Antonia Darder, perhaps the foremost scholar on the relationship between culture and language, references "linguistic genocide" as the outcome of marginalizing indigenous peoples' languages. She makes this claim regarding the power dynamics in language acceptance: "… the coloniality of power persists long after the initial colonizing moment, anchoring the hegemonic language within the universal eugenic claim that its epistemology is uniquely superior and the highest cognitive formulation of human existence" (Darder, 2015). She references her point to schooling:

> As such, U.S. education is part of a persistent colonial web. Accordingly, students' cultural and linguistic allegiances are eroded, as the "official" language, culture and identity of the nation-state is reinforced. In the process, hegemonic language practices thwart voice, self-determination, and social agency. (Darder, 2015)

Louis Moll (2010), in a lecture entitled, "Mobilizing Culture, Language, and Educational Practices: Fulfilling the Promises of Mendez and Brown," asserts:

> For so-called minority children, especially in the contemporary social context, educational resources and opportunities must include integrating their language and cultural experiences into the social and intellectual fabric of schools, much as these have always been seamlessly integrated into the education of privileged White children. In education, power is transmitted through these social relations, representations, and practices, which determine whose language and culture experiences count and whose do not, which students are at the center, and, therefore, which must remain in the periphery.

In "The Right (Write) Start: African American Language and the Discourse of Sounding Right," Dyson and Smitherman (2009) posit that in order

> ... to find their way into writing, children depend on the familiar and typified voices of their everyday lives – the voices of families, friends, media figures, teachers. These voices literally reverberate in their own as the children orally articulate what they are going to say and monitor its encoding on the page ... a curricular and pedagogical knowledge of young children's languages is important to identifying and helping young children meet the challenges they experience in figuring out how to make a voice visible on paper. (p. 3)

In a monstrous assault on linguistic democracy, the South African authorities used violence to declare language dominance. In June of 1976, fifteen thousand South African school children protested the imposition of the policy that would make English and Afrikaans the dual medium of instruction in classrooms across the country, in spite of the home languages of the youngsters. Petitions and pleadings by parents and teachers were ignored by the authorities. What started as a peaceful demonstration erupted into a violent confrontation when tear gas was used by the police. Hector Pieterson, not yet 13-years-old, was mortally wounded – hundreds of others were wounded as well – when police opened fire with live ammunition. The incident reverberated throughout the country, signaling the start of a young people's rebellion (Mandela, 1994). (You can find more about the Hector Pieterson incident in Chapter 5.)

Subreenduth (2013) points out the confusing and corrupting influence of choices for school language, i,e., the medium of instruction, in South African schools post-apartheid. A policy change in 1995 offered localized "control" over the medium of instruction, based on the dominant language in the locale of the school. But, this was a pyrrhic victory at best since the dominant languages of the country are English and Afrikaans, the languages of money and power.

Xhosa was Nelson Mandela's language as a child. It is one of the country's 11 official languages – which include English and Afrikaans, the languages of the colonizers. English and Afrikaans are used in the classrooms of South Africa as the preferred languages of instruction and are the prominent languages used in the best universities. I have witnessed the uphill struggle for both teacher and student in many of the township schools where the dominant language of the local community may be Zulu and students are taught in English or Afrikaans.

In a powerful indictment of the colonial powers that confiscated land from native peoples, Breda (2019) argues that the Khoe, The "First People" of South Africa, had their ancestral memories, identities and history erased. The worst offense was the erasure of language.

> Language is more than just the collection of signs and words we use. It informs our existence, guides us in foreign space, helps us understand the world we inhabit, helps us heal when hurt. Language is identity, language is heritage, language is culture. So what happens to you as a person, to your group, when those sacred words are taken away? And not just taken away, but by force and sheer brutality .... They say that when a language dies, it's like a museum that burns to the ground. (p. 9)

Notes

1   Ruth Anne Olson and Peggy McIntosh are contributors to *Beyond Heroes and Holidays: A Practical Guide to K-12 Anti-Racist Multicultural Education and Staff Development*. Olson has transduced the McIntosh generic list of white privilege benefits, one that has been widely circulated and praised, into a more focused list applied to the educational setting

2   Harber's article originally appeared in the *Journal of Educational Psychology*, 2012.

CHAPTER 5

Segregation: The Ghosts of de Jure, the Pervasiveness of de Facto

It is very appropriate that from this cradle of the Confederacy, this very heart of the great Anglo-Saxon Southland, that today we sound the drum for freedom as have our generations of forebears before us time and again down through history. Let us rise to the call for freedom-loving blood that is in us and send our answer to the tyranny that clanks its chains upon the South. In the name of the greatest people that have ever trod this earth, I draw the line in the dust and toss the gauntlet before the feet of tyranny, and I say *segregation now, segregation tomorrow and segregation forever.*

GEORGE WALLACE,[1] First Inaugural Speech as Governor of Alabama (1963)

• • •

Eie volk, eie taal, eie land [Our own people, our own language, our own land]
Die wit man moet altyd baas wees [The White man must always remain boss]

Nationalist slogans, South Africa

• •
•

Perhaps there is no construct more closely associated with racial bias than segregation. As noted in earlier chapters, humans are a tribal species, suspecting "others" will do them harm. As such, we cluster together with those who seem safe and segregate ourselves from others whom we fear. This ethos has driven our plans to claim territory for our own kind, plans that are endemic to society even today.

Arrangements for segregation have come under fire from "civilized" nations. Both South Africa and the United States have forsworn their allegiances to segregation by law, i.e., "de jure segregation" – a segregation that relegated people of color to second class citizenship with no entitlement to coveted spaces occupied by Whites. However, silhouettes of this "bygone" era are found

© KONINKLIJKE BRILL NV, LEIDEN, 2020 | DOI: 10.1163/9789004444430_005

everywhere – in both countries – hidden behind scheming rhetoric and political gamesmanship. These strategies serve to perpetuate the divisions that were once codified. If all else fails, then a new remedy – to keep the old order – rescues the privileged from the damnation of equality. De facto segregation permeates the landscapes of both countries. Segregation, "in fact" exists and is apparent to even the most casual observer, especially in the contested spaces in living arrangements and school demographics.

1   The Good Neighbor Policy

Robert Frost (b. 1874), the acclaimed American poet, in his plaintive poem, *Mending Wall*, asks what the purpose of a wall is. "Before I built a wall I'd ask to know. What I was walling in or walling out, And to whom I was like to give offence." His neighbor answers with a lesson he learned from his father. "Good fences make good neighbours." George Herbert (b. 1593), the Welsh-born poet, orator, and priest of the Church of England agrees: "Love your neighbor, yet pull not down your hedge." Seems the poets' reflections are widely followed in larger arenas.

South African Prime Minister Hendrik Verwoerd (1958–1966), regarded as the "architect" of apartheid, and, some would argue, the sanitizer-in-chief, shared this perspective at a rally:

> Our policy is one which is called by an Afrikaans word, "Apartheid." And, I am afraid that has been misunderstood so often. It could just as easily, and perhaps much better, be described as a policy of good neighborliness, accepting that there are differences between people. But while these differences exist and you have to acknowledge them, at the same time you can live together, give aid to one another, and that can best be done as good neighbors always do.[2]

In a comment about what had been called the "apartheid wall" in Israel, a wall built by Israel to separate Israeli citizens from non-citizens, a journalist from the Long Island newspaper *Jewish Star* offered this perspective:

> Every country in the world has different rules for citizens and non-citizens. That's not apartheid. That's not segregation. It's rule of law. What would be the point of citizenship if non-citizens were governed by the same regulations? The fact that Israel spends millions of shekels building roads for Palestinian Arabs is a remarkable act of generosity. The interna-

tional community should be heaping praise on Israel, not harassing the Jewish state with lies about 'apartheid.' (Flatow, 2019)

As I made my way to various schools in both South Africa and the US, I was confronted, quite often, with a stratagem used by administrators and parents alike who did not want to admit they were exclusionary. They insisted that all were welcome, including students of color. With a caveat or two.

When visiting a school in South Africa, one that has a distinguished reputation burnished regularly by accomplishments in scholarship, athletics, and donor largesse, I asked the headmaster how many students of color were enrolled in the school of 1,500. His answer was "about 15." When I questioned why there were so few, given the fact that a township filled with kids of color was nearby, he responded: "Anyone can come to this school, if they have the tuition and they can speak Afrikaans." Similarly, as I travel to locations in the United States, particularly in the richer areas in the New York vicinity, the managers and trustees of school districts will offer the same pledge as their South African counterparts, i.e., anyone can go to our schools, as long as they live in this neighborhood – where prices often start at one million dollars per home. (The scheme is similar to South Africa's "feeder zone" concept, mentioned later in the chapter.)

No discussion of a "wall" should exclude mention of the Presidency of Donald Trump, which has been characterized by many as the most divisive presidency in recent memory. Trump's dream of a wall on the US southern border separating Mexico from the US provided energy to those who believe this is necessary to keep the foreigners separated from the citizens. In this case, no pretense is made about being good neighbors. This worldwide phenomenon exposes the raw animus towards – and suspicion of – the "other."

Groups of people who have been "otherized" by the majority are likely to live outside the gates of the privileged. If they do, somehow, make it past the gate by presenting the requisite tickets to success, what will life be like in this new assemblage? The answer, in some cases, is unexpected, but perhaps not surprising.

Many people of color have decided to stay within their "sector" for reasons of belongingness. The Sabir family, of Milwaukee, Wisconsin, in the US, is one example. Joanne and Maanaan Sabir, both 37, had achieved much in their lives – attaining advanced college degrees, earning six figure incomes. After purchasing and living for a time in an expensive home in an upscale neighborhood, they decided to move to an all-Black neighborhood with high poverty and crime rates. Why? Because they felt more welcome there, more comfortable with their neighbors, and more accepted by them. The story reflects a trend wherein successful Black families choose to live in poor and segregated communities despite having the resources to move elsewhere. "It a national phenomenon challenging the popular assumption that segregation is more about class than about race, that when Black families earn more money, some ideal of post-racial integration will inevitably be reached" (Eligon & Gebeloff, 2016).

2   Enemy inside the Wire

"The wire," in military slang, is the fortified perimeter around a patrol base. To be "inside the wire" is to be safe. "Outside the wire" is where the enemy lurks, danger prevails, and battles are staged. In 2012, during the conflict between Afghanistan and the United States, a major breach of the perimeter occurred when fifteen Taliban, dressed as American soldiers, snuck into an air force base. A bloody confrontation ensued as a result of a catastrophic lapse in security – a rupture in the wire.

South Africa and the United States have established their own internal "wires." These Maginot lines, based on social hierarchy, are designed to defend the privileged from enemy combatants. In South Africa, especially in the more affluent areas, barbed wire and electrified fences are a common perimeter accouterment. As I walk around the city of Stellenbosch I am struck by the number of these fortresses; it seems that every domicile in the White area has this equipment. In the United States, a more civilized form of perimeter protection for the well-to-do is the "gated" community. In this instance, outsiders who wish to enter a residential complex must first stop at a toll booth-like house replete with a crossing barrier and a security guard tasked with keeping out the undesirables.

While electrified fences and security personnel presage an impending physical threat, more systemic approaches, deeply rooted in the racist lineage of both South Africa and the United States, were – and are – employed to ensure segregation. In the United States, the strategy of "redlining" was a notorious scheme wherein the powerful looked out for each other's property interests, abiding the notion that state-sanctioned racism was justified. In South Africa, the Group Areas Act served a similar purpose, going so far as to forcefully and unapologetically relocate the undesirables. A brief overview of these racially-charged inventions provides a glimpse into the machinations of privileged White communities to protect themselves from their putative enemy.

2.1   *Redlining*

In 1917, when the US Supreme Court ruled zoning laws that excluded Black people were unconstitutional, homeowners quickly came up with an alternative. They would create racially restrictive covenants between one another that would ban the sale of property to undesirable racial groups. According to one estimate, 80% of the neighborhoods in Chicago and Los Angeles had racially restrictive covenants by 1940. The Court, acting again in 1947, banned these covenants, but the practice had become so widespread that it was difficult to eliminate (Lockwood, 2019).

The federal government became involved in housing with the creation of the Federal Housing Administration (FHA) in 1934. This initiative was designed to shore up the housing market following the Great Depression. But instead of opening pathways for all Americans, the FHA used restrictive covenants as the paradigm for loan approval. The FHA, along with the federally funded Home Owners' Loan Coalition (HOLC), introduced "redlining" in over 200 American cities. HOLC created what were known as residential security maps, with different colors indicating which neighborhoods would be sound investments and which should be avoided. The descriptions of the demarcations are as chilling as they are diabolical (Lockwood, 2019).

Green ("Best"): Green areas represented in-demand, up-and-coming neighborhoods where "professional men" lived. These neighborhoods were explicitly homogenous, lacking "a single foreigner or Negro."

Blue ("Still Desirable"): These neighborhoods had "reached their peak" but were thought to be stable due to their low risk of "infiltration" by non-White groups.

Yellow ("Definitely Declining"): Most yellow areas bordered Black neighborhoods. They were considered risky due to the "threat of infiltration of foreign-born, Negro, or lower grade populations."

Red ("Hazardous"): Red areas were neighborhoods where "infiltration" had already occurred. These neighborhoods, almost all of them populated by Black residents, were described by the HOLC as having an "undesirable population" and were ineligible for FHA backing.

The impact of redlining can be felt today in corridors throughout the nation where decaying urban centers meet thriving suburban locales, despite passage of the Fair Housing Act of 1968, prohibiting redlining. The law may have changed, but the map is still color-coded.

The suburban communities in the US are particularly wary of incursions by people of color. A prime example is a delightful village, about a half hour car ride from New York City. An appeal of a court case from 2005 (in which the village was cited for responding favorably to residents who were resisting "multi-family" housing) is revealing.

> Using what the appeals court called code words, residents said that multifamily housing would change the 'flavor' and 'character' of the village and would lead to '4–10 people in an apartment,' and demanded a guarantee that the housing be 'upscale.' (Foderaro, 2016)

The judges wrote: "The tenor of the discussion at public hearings ... shows that citizen opposition, though not overtly race-based, was directed at a potential influx of poor, minority residents." The appeals court referenced what they called "code words" for the introduction of such housing (Foderaro, 2016).

I was escorting a colleague from the University of Stellenbosch on a tour of the Nassau County region – which so happens to be the county in which my university resides. We stopped on a street in a town – infamous for its poor living conditions, unsafe streets and deplorable schools – which happens to be contiguous to the wealthy White village referred to above. From where we stood, in the poor community, we could see a concrete landscape dominated by apartments above stores in chockablock arrangement. Our vantage point also afforded us a view of the wealthy community – tree-lined streets, enormous houses and large, manicured properties, a short distance up the road. The difference was shocking. At that moment, we realized we were observing the fruits of American apartheid.

Nassau County, where there are many wealthy communities, has a reputation as one of the most segregated counties in the United States. The well-to-do village mentioned earlier is hardly the only town which has conspired to keep low income housing from being built within its boundaries. And, at times, other groups were victimized by housing bias in the same county.

Levittown, a Nassau County community built in the 1950s by the building firm Levitt and Sons (founded by Abraham Levitt and managed by his two sons), is sometimes referred to as the first suburb in America. It was designed to accommodate those seeking a lifestyle far from the urban center. Levittown also attracted veterans who were offered low interest mortgages guaranteed by the Veterans Administration.

While Levittown symbolized the start of a new era of home ownership in the US, it would also become known as a bastion of racial segregation. The first residents of the community signed an agreement known as a "restrictive covenant" which forbade occupancy of the home by any but the Caucasian race. This restriction was sanctioned by the Federal Housing Administration which would not offer mortgages to "mixed race" developments. At the time, this exclusionary approach had consequences for Jews as well. While considered "White," Jews were still not welcome in the community. The sting of being one of the "not wanted" became personal for me.

My family moved from an apartment in Brooklyn, to a large, corner plot home in Levittown, across the street from the elementary school I attended. My father, as promised, benefited because of his vet status. We were thrilled with our new house in the "burbs." It was not long before things turned sour. At a "welcome wagon" get together, my mother was assured by someone who did not know she was Jewish, that her family would be happy in their new community. The woman made this comment: "Good thing you're not Jewish. We don't really want that kind in this neighborhood." My family moved within six months.

Other municipalities on Long Island are equally remarkable for their segregation from one another. With apologies for mixing metaphors, these towns are less concerned with a perimeter breach than other towns because they have what amounts to a "firebreak" between neighborhoods. (A firebreak is a purposely created gap in a forest or wooded area to stop the spread of a fire.) As mentioned earlier, highways, railroad tracks, and main thoroughfares provide this type of break between the White communities and the Black communities. Again, the contrast between one side of the tracks and the other is appalling.

A recent development on Long Island – which became a highly publicized scandal – was the exposure of "steering" practices engaged in by real estate agents. In a special report covering three years and dozens of Long Island real estate agents, *Newsday,* the Long Island newspaper of record, uncovered evidence of "... widespread unequal treatment of minority potential home buyers and minority communities. The findings included evidence that potential home buyers were steered to neighborhoods based on race and that agents required preapproval for mortgages from Black customers but not Whites" (Roy, 2019).

Not far from Nassau County is the city of Yonkers. In 1988, the city was 85% White; the remainder of the residents were Black and Hispanic and lived in a housing project. A federal judge ordered 200 units of low-rise subsidized houses be built to blend into White neighborhoods. The order fomented a series of political wranglings in which the city almost went bankrupt fighting the order. A new mayor, at first pledging to fight the decree, did an about face and was quickly thrown out of office. Begrudgingly, the city began to integrate but became an "... obvious allegory for a world that a lot of people want to pretend is post-racial ..." (Kimmelman, 2015).

2.2   *The Group Areas Act*

In 1950, the Group Areas Act was installed by the apartheid government of South Africa. It mandated that there be segregation by race, based on apartheid classifications: African, Coloured, Indian, and White. The Act created zones in which only one group could reside. Violations of the law would be met with serious consequences of fines up to 200 pounds and/or prison terms of up to two years. A particularly brutal part of this signature act was the forced removal of people from a designated area. The GAA – as it is sometimes known – gave license for the authorities to destroy whole communities, the most infamous incident being the destruction of Sophiatown near Johannesburg. In 1955, 2,000 policemen began removing people from the area, eventually turning it into Triomf (Victory), a community for Whites only. Included in the shame-annals of South African history is the forced removal of people from "District Six." The area, which is situated in an extraordinarily beautiful space beneath Cape Town's Table Mountain and not far from the sea (today a mecca for tourists) was declared a Whites-only area and by 1982, 60,000 people were removed from their homes in District Six to grim townships in the Cape Flats.

As if the forced relocation of thousands of "objectionable" people – think families with children as you imagine the transfer – were not enough, the devious apartheid government gave ostensible "independence" – with limited "self-rule" – to the inhabitants of these new territories. In fact, the plan was designed to reduce the government's responsibility to provide services – electricity, water, schooling, hospitals, and more – to these areas. By 1983, more than 600,000 people throughout the country were forcibly removed from their homes, losing entitlements that citizens of South Africa might otherwise have.

Today, South Africa still suffers from the ravages of the Group Areas Act. The Black townships are overcrowded to a furious degree and typically do not have water, plumbing, or electricity resources available to individual homes, which are most often small, corrugated huts. As referenced earlier, these shacks are not far away from – in fact, sometimes contiguous to – resplendent homes and malls and hotels and other offerings for the wealthy residents of the area. Much like the United States, the segregation screams bias but is silenced by those who like it that way. A drive through the Western Cape area of South Africa, east of Cape Town, one finds a landscape of extraordinary beauty, offering panoramic views of some of the most magnificent mountain ranges in the world. In sharp contrast is the ugliness in living conditions on the ground.

The dismantling of the apartheid government has not led to the promise of equality for the people of South Africa. The situation is particularly disappointing to the "born frees," those who were born after 1994 when Nelson Mandela was sworn in as President and hope was on the rise for a more equitable society.

It is worth noting that today in South Africa there is a movement to expropriate the land seized by Whites under the imprimatur of the GAA. Throughout the country, incursions by Blacks into land held by Whites is on the rise. White farmers are in control of 70% of farms held by individual owners, although Whites account for less than 8% of the total population. In some areas – the Stellenbosch wine region is a prime example – squatters from township communities are building shacks on farms currently owned by White farmers. The Economic Freedom Fighters, an offshoot of the ANC, is encouraging Black South Africans to take back the land on their own. The dispute exposes afresh the wounds of the apartheid era. It remains to be seen how this latest development will impact the living situation as well as the political dynamics in the country (Gebrekidan & Onishi, 2019).

My personal journeys have taken me many times through these calculated divisions. Spending time in various locales – visiting homes, schools, neighborhoods, and chatting with people from all backgrounds – I have been astounded by the differences in lifestyle I observe. I have attempted, throughout my travels in South Africa, to remain fully cognizant of my own country's abhorrent policies, and aware of my own privilege as a White person. I offer this declaration not only for the reader, but as a reminder to myself.

3   Separate and Unequal Schools

One common thread, whether I'm reporting on poverty in New York City or in Sierra Leone, is that good education tends to be the most reliable escalator out of poverty. Another common thread: whether in America or Africa, disadvantaged kids often don't get a chance to board that escalator. (Nicholas Kristoff,[3] journalist)

3.1   *Antecedents*
The antecedents to the present day segregation iteration in both the United States and South Africa are legion. The long and tumultuous histories of the nations are rife with examples of racial segregation battles which are often

showcased in educational settings. The inflection points in these narratives are enshrined in high profile legal cases and social movements. They provide a backdrop for the continuing discussions of inequality in schooling and a window into how the challenges produce tortured logic.

3.2   *The United States*

The imprimatur for the infamous "separate but equal" doctrine was granted by the US Supreme Court in 1896. The case, *Plessy v. Ferguson*, was borne of an inquiry into the meaning of the Fourteenth Amendment's (1868) equal-protection clause, which prohibits states from denying "equal protection of the laws" to all persons under their jurisdiction. In an artfully designed premise, the case gave sanction to laws which promoted racial segregation, as long as resources were equally provided for both Whites and African Americans. It took over half a century for the ruling to be overturned by the Supreme Court in *Brown v. Board of Education.*

The 1954 case, the most celebrated milestone in the struggle for the desegregation of schools, *Brown v. BOE,* asserted that African-American children in the Topeka, Kansas, school system were denied access to all-White schools and therefore, were denied equality of educational services. The plaintiffs argued that separate but equal is inherently unequal. Most interesting, perhaps, is the underlying premise of the argument: "The Court determined that separate schools, even if they had similar resources, were 'inherently' – by their nature – unequal, causing profound damage to the children who attended them and hobbling their ability to live as full citizens of the country" (Hannah-Jones, 2016). (The potency of *Brown v. BOE* is questioned by some who wonder if students of color really benefit from the law, a perspective discussed earlier.)

Affirmative action, a policy borne of strictures in the 1964 Civil Rights Act, was designed to create opportunities for traditionally marginalized groups. Businesses, colleges, and other institutions participate in this initiative. Grants, scholarships, and other financial supports are provided for underrepresented students applying to colleges. Business hiring practices often require a pool of candidates for a job opening be from a variety of backgrounds or a business risks losing federal funding or eligibility for federal contracts.

The Bakke decision (1978) challenged the affirmative action system by citing the illegitimacy of quotas used in all circumstances in the Medical School of the University of California at Davis application procedure. In the practice, 16 out of every 100 seats in an entering class were reserved for "Blacks," Chicanos," "Asians," and "American Indians." Allan Bakke sued the university when he was (twice) rejected from admission, demonstrating that his academic qualifications were better than those minorities who were accepted. In a 5–4 decision, the US Supreme Court ruled that race could be a factor in admissions criteria, but only if weighed in conjunction with other criteria and determined on a case-by-case basis. The court ruled against the university, citing that its policy violated the Constitution's Equal Protection Clause.[4]

3.3   *South Africa*

Sometimes referred to as the Native Education Act, the Bantu Education Act of 1953 segregated an already segregated South African education system even more so. Its design was to guarantee that certain people would be ill-equipped to take a productive place in society at large. (The Department of Native Affairs, headed by Hendrik Verwoerd, the "architect of apartheid," oversaw Black South African education.) The Bantu Education Act's poisonous entrails have remained in the circulatory system of the South African culture for decades, undermining opportunities and life chances for Black people. Lehola describes the damage:

> Differences in intergenerational mobility have remained significant across population groups. The same families tend to constitute the most educated group from one generation to the next. Economists refer to this as the under-education trap, as some families remain unskilled from one generation to the next. (as cited in Motlanthe, 2013, pp. 11–12)

The end of the apartheid era (1994) signaled the "official" end of racial categorizations in South Africa. In a spirit of reimagining the country, new paradigms were introduced to foreclose on the existing ones. But, much like in the United States, there was a tension created between those who would call on the state to make redress for past injustices and those who espoused the concept of non-racialism. A heated policy debate in the University of Cape Town provides a laboratory for examining these competing forces.

In 2010, University of Cape Town professors, 70% of whom were White at the venerable institution which, during the apartheid era, admitted few students of color (those who were admitted were prohibited from dormitories and other campus facilities) voted to support a policy, much like the US policy of affirmative action, which would give preference in admissions to students who were classified by the apartheid categories as Black, mixed race, and Indian. In doing so they were supporting the movement to redress the sins of apartheid as they impacted education.

Some students of color balked at the initiative, one asking, "Are we here because we're Black or are we here because we're intelligent?" Intense debate was triggered, with opponents firmly in two camps. One perspective, expressed by Professor Neville Alexander, a highly-regarded sociologist, was that the policy of affirmative action undermines the progress that was supposed to accompany the dissolution of apartheid. He contended that the concept of non-racialism, a principle that those in the anti-apartheid struggled, fought, and died for, is compromised by the university policy. Alexander, who spent 10 years imprisoned on Robben Island with Nelson Mandela, took a hardline position regarding the university policy, as exemplified in this comment made at a public forum: "The government under apartheid did the same and we told them to go to hell" (Dugger, 2010). The chief champion on campus of affirmative action was Vice Chancellor Max Price. He exhorted campus policy makers to resist calls for affirmative action to be abolished. His contention was that the policy gave, at the very least, opportunities to those who were handicapped by governmental policy. Price was, himself, a White anti-apartheid student activist in the 1970's (Dugger, 2010).

Carter (2012) explicates the dilemma succinctly:

> Some argue that the abstract ideal of non-racialism that has served post-apartheid South Africa has run up against the imperatives of *transformation,* leading to a more messy terrain, where race has been constitutionally outlawed as a moral basis for citizenship and inclusion in the political sphere. Yet, legislatively, race is inscribed for strategic purposes of redress. (p. 180)

This internecine conflict continues to vex the progress towards an egalitarian society. Carter continues:

> Frequently, I found students and educators expressing concrete beliefs that exposed a type of 'laissez-faire' approach to the reduction of inequality. 'The government should not do anything to specifically redress past inequality. Rather let the past rest,' they might say. (p. 180)

3.4 *The More Things Change in the Policy Initiatives Ether, the More They Stay the Same on the Ground*

In both the United States and South Africa, the wounds of the racial divide have been festering despite efforts to heal them. Data, research, and disturbing examples regarding education testify to the bleak contours of the situation.

Apartheid in South Africa, the official government guiding principle for decades, left a trail of social maladies, no more apparent, perhaps, than in the school setting. The trend line of school attendance – from 2002–2012 (Lehohla, 2013) – reveals a huge dip in school attendance in Black and Coloured communities after ages 15 and 16. The role of basic education, of course, has a serious impact on the economic stability of a country. A Stats SA report titled, "Education Series III: Educational enrollment and achievement, 2016," states:

Differences in intergenerational mobility have remained significant across population groups. The same families tend to constitute the most educated group from one generation to the next. Economists refer to this as the under-education trap, as some families remain unskilled from one generation to the next. (Motlanthe, 2013, p. 11)

The National Planning Commission – or NPC – found that: "Education and skills remain at the heart of the country's employment crisis. The lack of opportunities to enter the workforce to gain experience, coupled with the poor schools' education and limited networks, consigns many young work-seekers to long-term unemployment" (Lehohla, 2018, p. 116). South Africa's school system is characterized by extreme inequalities, from expensive private-sector schools offering excellent education to no-fee pubic-sector schools where a worthwhile education is dubious. The NPC emphatically states "the quality of education for most Black children is poor" (Lehohla, 2018, p. 116).

Nic Spaull, a university professor and researcher of socio-economic issues, and a widely recognized social science expert, has examined schooling disparities in South Africa between rich and poor. In an article in South Africa's *The Sunday Times* (2015), he excoriates the design of the public school system, i.e., the Quintile System, in which schools are classified into five categories ranging from no fee schools to tuition-based schools. The tuition-based schools are progressively more expensive. Spaull submits that "It is an unspoken truth that no-fee schools are for the poor and 'good' schools are for the rich" (Spaull, 2015). No fee schools make up the vast majority of South African schools. Not surprisingly, children in these schools are less likely to attend higher education institutions. Spaull (2015) exclaims:

After 21 years of democratic rule, most Black children still receive an education that condemns them to the underclass of South African society, where poverty and unemployment are the norm. This substandard education does not develop their capabilities or expand their economic opportunities: instead, it denies them dignified employment and undermines their sense of self-worth.

Spaull explains another devious practice, this one designed to exclude children who cannot pay fees, i.e., mostly children of color, from certain schools. There exist informal mechanisms for exclusion, including biased interview policies, long waiting lists, and "feeder zones." The latter allows schools to define the geographic areas from which the school children will be accepted, usually a few kilometers from their school. The Group Areas Act is resurrected in this strategy by giving former 'White' schools in 'White' neighborhoods the right to select students from the locales adjacent to the school because they live in the school's "feeder zone."

Children in no fees schools are often targets of both school employee and parental neglect and abuse. Commenting (in the *Weekend Argus*) on a case involving charges of sexual abuse of students by a former assistant principal, the principal of a primary school in the township of Masiphumelele, said that children in his school were vulnerable because of "dire financial circumstances and that 'ignorant parents' had no interest in taking care of them" (Schroeder, 2015). He added that there were many child-headed households in the community and sometimes abusers promised money to the children. He insisted that the school did try to address the issues by educating the children about potential dangers, but there was little the school could do once the children went home at the end of the day (Schroeder, 2015).

The cloud hanging over the South African social landscape, much like the "blanket" that hangs over Table Mountain when clouds move in, obscures the vision of those who, in earnest, want to rise above it. The incorporeal specter of apartheid remains. This is the case in higher education environments as well.

A Ph.D. student at the University of Stellenbosch, (a university once referred to as "the cradle of apartheid") shares that she is often uncomfortable as a Black female student in the prestigious White-majority school, including times when she walks in the neighborhood of the school. While she says she has gained a lot from policies such as affirmative action, she nevertheless feels the weight of her country's apartheid history in her daily experiences as she attempts to fit into settings where there are only a few Black people (Shabalala, 2018).

My consciousness about these issues was often penetrated by my own experiences in Stellenbosch, in visits to both the town and the university. On one occasion, I observed a university class discussing the history of colonial tyranny against natives. This most important message, how centuries before the country was subjected to Whites claiming their sovereignty over the Blacks (and their right to confiscatory acquisitions of resources) was being delivered in the University of Stellenbosch, one of the most prestigious institutions in all of Africa, in a country whose population is nearly 90% Black and Coloured, in a lecture hall filled with virtually all White students!

One Sunday morning I attended a service in a church adjacent to the university. The sermon was stirring. Hundreds of congregants sang the hymn, "River of Peace," which includes the lines: "I'll sing of a river divine/Its waters from trouble release/More precious than 'honey and wine,'/That river, sweet river of peace." While I have no doubt that these young parishioners, most of whom were university students, were sincere in their faith, I was struck – and deeply disturbed – by the incongruity of the moment. A spiritual message about divine, sweet rivers which deliver us from trouble, was being sung by a room packed with *all* White students – *I did not see one person of color in the room* – in a land that has been hobbled by a maelstrom of racial unrest for centuries and blighted by continuing hate based on skin color.

The United States has been home to enormous contradictions between purported changes and actual circumstances. In her groundbreaking study, "Why Boundaries Matter," Amy Stuart Wells (2009) unpacks the baked-in damage done by segregating school systems in the United States. She uses Long Island, New York, for the location of her study. She reminds us that this region is "... home to some of the most fragmented, segregated and unequal school districts in the United States ..." (Wells, 2009). She speaks of the relationship between "place" and "opportunity" where place is determined by race and wealth. She asserts that "separate can never be equal" because of this relationship. "The boundaries divide areas by property values, tax rates, public revenues, private resources, working conditions, family income and wealth, parental educational levels, and political clout" (Wells, 2009). She continues: "The fact that these disparities are so starkly defined by race/ethnicity and social class should give us pause in a country that likes to think of itself as 'post-racial' and 'colorblind'" (Wells, 2009).

Elaine Gross, President of *ERASE Racism*, Long Island's premier advocacy group working to improve race relations, reinforces the Wells study by pointing out that segregation in Long Island public schools has only gotten worse from 2004–2016. The number of "intensely segregated school district (90–100% non-White) more than doubled, and students attending these segregated schools more than tripled" (Gross, 2018).

Hannah-Jones (2016) exposes the troubling circumstances of education for children in New York City, home to more than one million public school students. Half of the White children (who represent just 15% of the overall public school population) are housed in 11% of the schools. In a "carefully curated integration" these schools have some students of color. This, so parents can "boast that their children's public schools look like the United Nations ..." (Hannah-Jones, 2016). The flip side of the demographic is that Black and Latino children in New York City are isolated, with 85% of Black students and 75% of Latino students attending "intensely" segregated schools with White populations of less than 10%.

Despite official ratification of protective laws against discrimination and condemnation of continuing discrimination from the highest levels of government, the everyday lives of some citizens are privileged because of their backgrounds. Is genuine integration, in effect, a pipedream of those who seek social justice? It appears that way to many.

4   In the US, It's Race to the Bottom

Beneath hypocritical politesse, lies the ugly underbelly of racism. Here reside the unapologetic voices which sustain inequality, sow division and, at times, turn to violence to make their point.

In the United States, there has been a shameful gallery of incidents. Nikole Hannah-Jones,[5] in an OpEd in *The New York Times* (2019), ticks off a sample of the obscenities.

In 1964, in New York City, a walkout was organized by almost a half million Black and Puerto Rican students, in response to conditions where White schools remained segregated from Black schools, despite activist attempts to desegregate the schools. White schools were half-empty and minority schools were severely overcrowded through a policy of racial assignment. In a token response to the protest, the city agreed to a very limited desegregation plan involving busing between 30 White schools and 30 Black and Puerto Rican schools in a school system of one million students. This was followed by a protest from 10,000 White parents, mostly women, who opposed "busing." Not to be confused with White Southerners who used racially charged language to protest busing, the New York City protestors claimed they were fighting for their own civil rights – the right to send their children to a neighborhood school and not be bused elsewhere. The strategy worked. The national media who covered the event did so with a sympathetic ear.

In the 1970s in Boston, riots followed federal court orders mandating that Black children be bused to White areas. Black children were assaulted by rock-throwing White adults, who beat them and called them "niggers." It was clear that the fight was not about White children being allowed to go to their neighborhood schools. That's where they already were.

In 1981, Lee Atwater, the darling of Republican strategists at the time, offered this advice to White folks as they set about undermining desegregation: "You start out in 1954 by saying, 'Nigger, nigger, nigger.' By 1968 you can't say 'nigger' – that hurts you, backfires. So you say stuff like, uh, 'forced busing,' 'states' rights' and all that stuff."

Hannah-Jones (2014) chronicled the sad circumstances surrounding the tragedy of a Black student, Michael Brown, who attended Normandy High School in St. Louis, Missouri. He had just graduated high school in the summer of 2014 when he was killed in nearby Ferguson, by a White police officer. The incident gained national attention and sparked a debate about race, policing, and justice. Part of the discussion centered around a long and infamous trail of opposition in the St. Louis community to desegregation initiatives. In 2009, Normandy's schools, which were struggling to meet minimum requirements, were ordered to absorb students from the Wellston schools. Wellston was an all-Black district with conditions that state officials called "deplorable" and "academically abusive." Despite the fact that there were many White, high-performing school districts not far from Wellston, the decision was made to combine it with another challenging environment. Things changed – for a moment – when the Normandy district was deemed so poor that it lost its accreditation status, which meant that, by state law, students in Normandy could transfer to an accredited district. That's when the White folks' alarm bells went off.

Francis Howell, an 85% White district 26 miles away, was chosen to receive Normandy's students. A public meeting was held in the Howell district to respond to community concerns. What transpired was, sadly, not unexpected. More than 2,500 parents showed up to a meeting in the high school gym. Questions and comments from the audience included: "Would the district install metal detectors? What about the violence their children would be subjected to, an elementary school parent asked. Wouldn't test scores plummet? The issue wasn't about race, one parent said, 'but trash'" (Hannah-Jones, 2014). And, a young girl in the audience, one of the few brown faces, wiped away tears as she said, "It made me heartbroken because they were putting us in a box. I was sitting there thinking, 'Would you want some other parents talking about your kid that way?'" (Hannah-Jones, 2014).

In 2010, Eden Prairie, Minnesota, attempted to redistribute populations in their five elementary schools to reduce the enrollment imbalance – some schools were overcrowded and others were underused. In addition to this goal, school officials wanted to integrate minority children (who were concentrated in one school) throughout the district. The remaining four schools were populated by largely White and affluent students. Cries of "forced busing" and "social engineering" were heard from parents in the White communities in blogs, Facebook posts, letters to the editor, and at public meetings. One parent commented in a local newspaper: "I will not have my kids going to school with gang members and guns." Often the sentiments were accompanied by the shibboleth, "This has nothing to do with race" (Eaton, 2012).

Flat-out racial animus – that I have experienced or that has been relayed to me by others whom I know well – remains raw within my personal storehouse of memories. Examples, described below, will hopefully further the narrative about the racial divide.

A friend who lives in a neighboring town in Nassau County – my current place of residence – shared with me how certain groups in his community express their resentment. There are approximately 50% White and 50% Black and Latino residents living in the neighborhood, which is geographically segregated by race, many of the wealthier Whites living near the shoreline. He told me that he only sees White people when they come out to vote "No" on the public school budget, most of them sending their children to private schools.

Even when it can be shown that a White community will have a tangible reward if it combines with a Black community, the answer will still be a resounding no. In the late 1990s on Long Island, I experienced racist vitriol first hand when an idea was circulating that two nearby school districts should merge. One was a mostly White community and the other almost exclusively Black. The rationale was not only to address the immorality of segregation, but to reap the benefits of the financial gain. (Merging districts would save considerable tax money on administrative and capital costs.) Despite the demonstrated monetary benefit, the White community was up in arms. The petitions circulating contained vile remarks about the negative influence the Black students would have on the White students. The lobby prevailed. The districts are still separated to this day.

To be painfully honest, my social justice leanings are sometimes trumped by my cravings for comfort, as in this story that troubles me to this day.

When my children were in elementary school, we built a house in a new development in a municipality. The community was in the perfect spot for us – not far from my children's school. All new homes on a beautiful tract of land was just the place for us. One day, as the construction was ongoing, I was in the builder's office and I noticed there was a Black couple sitting at his desk reviewing the house plans in this new neighborhood. After they left, my wife and I sat down at his desk. He volunteered: "I spoke with those people, but I will make sure not to sell them a house. The other new people will come after me with baseball bats if I do." (We continued to build the house and lived in it for nearly 20 years.)

5   South Africa Opens Fire

South Africa's history of school troubles based on race is most notorious for the ghastly Hector Pieterson incident.

Hector Pieterson, a 12-year old who participated in the 1976 Soweto uprising to protest the edict that the sole medium of instruction in South African schools should be Afrikaans, became the iconic figure for the anti-apartheid movement. Hector was one of the first casualties when police were ordered to open fire on what was a peaceful protest up to that point. Ten people died and 250 were injured in the assault. June 16, the day of the incident, has been observed as the public holiday known as "Youth Day" since 1994. A photo of Hector dying in the arms of a classmate who is struggling to help him was released worldwide. It's heartbreaking message was a clarion call to all nations to view South African apartheid with a more critical eye.

I visited the Hector Pieterson Museum on one of my visits to Soweto. The area, not far from where the original incident took place, includes the Hector Pieterson Memorial and has been declared a national heritage site. The museum contains photos, oral testimonies, audiovisual displays, and documents related to the events. The story the museum artifacts convey is breathtaking in its vulgarity. Sam Nzima's iconic photograph of Hector is displayed at the memorial in Soweto. Nzima commented on the moment:

> I saw a child fall down. Under a shower of bullets I rushed forward and went for the picture. It had been a peaceful march, the children were told to disperse, they started singing Nkosi Sikelele. The police were ordered to shoot. (Solar, 2013)

The children were singing the Black national anthem (officially recognized in 1991) of South Africa, a verse of which is:

> *Sounds the call to come together,*
> *And united we shall stand,*
> *Let us live and strive for freedom,*
> *In South Africa our land.*

When visiting the Hector Pieterson Secondary School, which has become a regular stop on my South African sojourns, I am greeted by a giant, painted mural based on the celebrated photo. Its placement at the entrance to the school is a stark reminder of what happens when violence is unleashed upon children. The image has become a symbol of both oppression and courage for the nation.

Even after the horrors of the Hector Pieterson incident that rocked the con-science of the world, it is still true today that in many South African schools the language medium of instruction is Afrikaans. While there are 11 official languages in South Africa, most Black South African children do not speak Afrikaans and are therefore ineligible for admission to Afrikaans-medium schools. Since the School Governing Body (SGB) – similar to the Board of Education in the United States – determines the language of instruction, many choose Afrikaans so as to exclude certain native-tongue speakers. By doing so, these young people are, in effect, disenfranchised from the economic networks in the country, which are expressed in either English or Afrikaans. (Read more about language bias in Chapter 4.)

Notes

1 George Wallace was regarded by many as the chief spokesperson for maintaining the segregation paradigm in the United States. The excerpt here is from a (in)famous speech he delivered. The last several words are in bold print to reflect how the pitch and volume of his voice during the speech became bolder when he repeated his pledge to keep segregation alive.

2 Retrieved from https://www.youtube.com/watch?v=vPClngczoys

3 Kristoff has done work around the world exposing corruption and injustice, and has been a champion for victims of war, poverty and disease. This quote comes from one of his highly regarded and widely-read entries into the *NY Times* editorial pages (October 19, 2011).

4 The Bakke decision, a landmark case in US Supreme Court history, was equivocal. There was no single majority position. The court had it both ways: they agreed to honor affirmative action, but under the circumstances presented to them in this case, they agreed that racial quotas were not a sufficient reason to deny the plaintiff access to the university.

5 Nikole Hannah-Jones, an award-wining, investigative journalist, studies and writes about racial injustice for the *New York Times* magazine. She is the creator of the 1619 Project, which commemorates the 400th anniversary of the arrival of the first enslaved people from West Africa. The project examines the legacy of slavery and how it can be reframed to better understand the history and contributions of Black Americans.

CHAPTER 6

The "Bootstraps" Scold

> None of us got where we are solely by pulling ourselves up by our
> bootstraps. We got here because somebody – a parent, a teacher, an Ivy
> League crony or a few nuns – bent down and helped us pick up our boots.
>
> THURGOOD MARSHALL,[1] US Supreme Court Justice (1967–1991)

∴

Heated – and often raucous – public discourse has emerged around issues
of meritocracy. Should our cultural heritage and our life circumstances be
considered – for better or for worse – when we are evaluated for opportunities in
the wider world? Should we consider the conditions of our upbringings which
may have benefited those of us from privileged communities and militated
against those of us from marginalized communities? Will the privileged have a
"leg up" that propels them ahead of the rest of the pack simply because of their
inherited status? And, if so, how long will this generational boost be tolerated
by those left behind?

Some respond that our common humanity demands that we make allow-
ances for those less fortunate than others as they try to succeed. Others demand
a tougher standard, a "sink or swim" ethos, a "no excuses" imperative. These
"Horatio Alger" myth-subscribers insist that each person be responsible for his
or her own success regardless of background. This, despite the generational
replay of advantage for some and disadvantage for others. Often, as individuals enter the social circles of the outside world – neighborhoods, schools, the
workforce, etc. – those who are fortunate enough to be borne of privilege are
presumed worthy and those burdened by raw bias are subject to derision and
relegated to second-class status. An untoward reaction is all too commonplace
throughout the world.

Pick yourself up by your own bootstraps!

For those struggling in this social tug-of-war in South Africa and the United
States, there are distinctive brandings of position.

© KONINKLIJKE BRILL NV, LEIDEN, 2020 | DOI: 10.1163/9789004444430_006

1 No Excuses

> There's a lack of moral, political, and intellectual integrity in [the] suppression of awareness of how social and economic disadvantage lowers achievement. Our first obligation should be to analyze social problems accurately; only then can we design effective solutions. Presenting a deliberately flawed version of reality, fearing that the truth will lead to excuses, is not only corrupt but also self-defeating. (Rothstein, 2008)

The knee jerk responses to those with little or no social capital who ask for assistance navigating the trials of assimilation are all too familiar. In his op-ed, "When Whites Just Don't Get It," Kristof (2014) shares reader responses to his charge of "smug White delusion" about race relations in America:

> Blacks don't get it ... Choosing to be cool vs. getting good grades is a bad choice. We all start from 0.

> Look, the basic reason young Black men are regarded with suspicion is that they are disproportionately criminals, The root problem isn't racism. It's criminality.

> Probably has something to do with their unwillingness to work.

In August 2019, Donald Trump's Acting Director of US Citizenship and Immigration Services weighed in with his opinion on taking care of the disenfranchised and less fortunate seeking assistance. He was asked whether or not the words of the poem, The New Colossus, emblazoned on the Statue of Liberty in New York harbor – *Give me your tired, your poor, your huddled masses yearning to be free as a welcome to those who seek shelter from harm* – were still valid. He responded: "They certainly are, with this modification: 'Give me your tired and your poor who can stand on their own two feet and who will not become a public charge'" (Martin & Ingber, 2019).

When educators fail to recognize that for some children, the edict "we'll take no excuses" is tantamount to "you must change who you are before we will accept your worthiness," we miss the opportunity to touch their lives positively and help them thrive if we ignore their lived realities. The problems are not in the children themselves; they are, after all, involuntary passengers on the troubled journeys of their families and unwitting victims of injustices in the wider environment.

In a piece entitled, *Overcoming the Challenges of Poverty*, Julie Landsman, a consultant on equitable education, shares a story told by a workshop participant, someone who teaches in a high poverty elementary school in the US. She described a moment in her class at 8 am when a kindergartner fell asleep at his seat. She began to talk loudly in his ear, until he awoke. Her rationale was that she taught in a "no excuses" school. A fellow teacher, who knew the student well, replied that the youngster lives in a homeless shelter and did not get to sleep until 4 am (Landsman, 2014).

In 1965, then US assistant labor secretary, Daniel Patrick Moynihan, popularized a famous (infamous?) concept known as "the culture of poverty," arguably placing the blame for the social ills of Black people on their own deficiencies. This notion – while since debunked by many social scientists – provides a convenient space for those who tarry in a narrative about the poor based on a "deficit" view.[2]

Teachers are not immune to such thinking.

In their study of the perceptions of White, experienced teachers on the lack of success of their students of color, McKenzie and Scheurich (2004) suggest that teachers are prone to "equity traps," which they define as "patterns of thinking and behavior that trap the possibilities for creating equitable schools for children of color" (p. 603). The first trap they identify is what they term "a deficit view," in which teachers attribute the lack of success of their students (of color) to "inherent or endogenous" deficiencies. Examples include: "cultural inadequacies, lack of motivation, poor behavior, or failed families and communities." These deficits are seen as generational, described by one teacher as a "culture of apathy." Some teachers went so far as to say that these students learn to misbehave from one another; one "infects" the next. Sometimes they referred to their students as "gangsters." Generally, teachers in the study felt that when four-year-olds walked into their classrooms they brought deficits with them that "teachers should not be expected to overcome."

Often we hear these sentiments expressed by Whites: "My parents never asked for a handout. How was I able to make it? For one thing, I didn't rely on excuses to run away from my responsibilities." As Collins and Jun (2017) see it:

> White people often respond to racialized pain with their own stories of hurt, pain, suffering and loss ... we have found that White pain and further identification with other systems of dominance based on identity markers around gender, class, ability status can be used as an attempt to delegitimize the pain that people of color endure within the systems of racialized oppression.

Conditions are worse in South Africa for many neighborhoods 25 plus years after the end of apartheid. As a South African principal shared: abuse, "gang-sterism," and child abuse are all on the rise in townships. The schools are still woefully inadequate in poor areas and abundantly resourced in wealthy areas. This, despite the quintile system wherein certain schools are designated "no fee" schools where the government underwrites expenses. Many well-to-do people say they are taking care of the poorest children by providing funds to the neediest schools, i.e., the model services the communities fairly. Many White people ask: Why are they holding on to apartheid when it was abolished long ago? McKaiser (2015) suggests the sentiment is: "What DO Black people want from me?"

Young White people in both countries often voice sentiments about troubling social dynamics. Carter (2012) interviewed students in both the United States and South Africa. She found what she calls "paradoxical, attitudinal value-behavior 'stretches.'"

> On the one hand, many agree that inequality and segregation are not healthy social phenomena. On the other hand, many care to do little to ameliorate these problems or to consider 'hitching the framing of these issues to the past.' 'Why am I supposed to feel some guilt, or be responsible for what happened in the past'?' (Carter, 2012)

In the United States, a sixteen-year-old White female student weighed in with her perspective on White people's responsibility:

> That's the only, like, I would have to say real problem, is just that they [Blacks], I think that like we owe them something, and it's like, okay ... it was like your great, great, great, great, great grandfather. Honestly. We're past that, but they [Blacks] still bring up. It's kind of ridiculous, I was like we were slaves first in Egypt, and we did it, so .... (Carter, 2012)

An ocean away, a White male high school student in South Africa had a similar take on letting go of past grievances. When asked what he would do to redress the legacy of apartheid, he said ...

> What I'd do is ... not necessarily forget about [it], but stop teaching it in schools. I know that from grade one, we get apartheid this and that – every single year. Just enforcing it, just enforcing it ... And the thing is that I feel that's, you know, there isn't racism as much between people now,

the youth today, like our generation because we haven't had that sort of thing. The only reason that it's there is because they keep on teaching it in schools .... (Carter, 2012)

2   When the Cards Are Stacked against You

The expression "the cards are stacked against you" originated in the gambling world. In a game of chance, the cards are "fixed" so that one player is at a disadvantage and it is impossible – or nearly impossible – for the disadvantaged player to win. The outside influence in the game determines the likelihood of the outcome. It seems the phrase was custom-built for characterizing racial and social inequalities. Representations are aplenty, both in non-fiction and fiction genres.

Louis Agassiz was a Swiss naturalist who emigrated to the United States in the 1840s and was the foremost spokesperson for polygeny, the theory that humans evolved from several different pairs of ancestors. He became a celebrated figure in the Harvard intellectual community. A sample of his attitudes, which were widely circulated, gives us a window into well-regarded positions at the time:

> It seems to us to be mock-philanthropy and mock-philosophy to assume that all races have the same abilities, enjoy the same powers, and show the same natural dispositions, and that in consequence of this equality they are entitled to the same position in human society. History speaks here for itself .... This compact continent of Africa exhibits a population which has been in constant intercourse with the White race, which has enjoyed the benefit of the example of the Egyptian civilization, of the Phoenician civilization and the Roman civilization, of the Arab civilization ... and nevertheless there has never been a regulated society of Black men developed on that continent. Does not this indicate in this race a peculiar apathy, a peculiar indifference to the advantages afforded by a civilized society? (Gould, 1981, p. 47)

In a peculiarly patronizing rant on "negro" deficiencies, he argues:

> Social equality I deem at all times impracticable. It is a natural impossibility flowing from the very character of the negro race [for Blacks are] indolent, playful, sensuous, imitative, subservient, good natured, versatile, unsteady on their purpose, devoted, affectionate, in everything unlike other races, they may but be compared to children, grown

> in the stature of adults while retaining a childlike mind .... (Gould, 1981,
> p. 46)

And, finally, he exhorts Whites to be cautious when considering granting privileges to the Blacks:

> No man has a right to what he is unfit to use ... Let us beware of granting
> too much to the negro race in the beginning, lest it become necessary
> to recall violently some of the privileges which they may use to our
> detriment and their own injury (10 August 1863). (Gould, 1981, p. 46)

In a parallel universe, on the same topic, nearly a century later, Alan Paton, in his manifesto on the South Africa racial divide, *Cry the Beloved Country*, composed this dialogue. It takes place in a courtroom drama about the dilemma of dealing with the "natives." Paton indicts the diabolical logic, vouchsafed by Whites, that suggests more education will mean a more intelligent (informed?) Black community, which will only increase their criminality (Paton, 1948). This exchange involves Mr. de Villiers, a proponent of underwriting school costs for native children, a chairman who is conducting the proceeding, and two interrogators, one of whom, Mr. Scott, suggests a "more schooling/more clever criminals" line of reasoning.
- And you think, Mr. de Villiers, that increased schooling facilities would cause a decrease in juvenile delinquency amongst native children?
- I am sure of it, Mr. Chairman.
- Have you the figures for the percentage of children at school, Mr. de Villiers?
- In Johannesburg, Mr. Chairman, not more than four out of ten are at school. But of those four not even one will reach his sixth standard. Six are being educated on the streets.
- May I ask Mr. de Villiers a question, Mr. Chairman?
- By all means, Mr. Scott
- Who do you think should pay for this schooling, Mr. de Villiers?
- We should pay for it. If we wait till native parents can pay for it, we will pay more heavily in other ways.
- Don't you think, Mr. de Villiers, that more schooling simply means cleverer criminals?

Here's PW Botha, South African Prime Minister from 1978–1984, channeling Paton:

> I am not against the provision of the necessary medical assistance to colored and natives, because unless they receive that medical aid, they become a source of danger to the European community. (Boddy-Evans, 2019)

Wealth disparity is the great divide which offers some a platform of resources to advance in a culture (whether they take the opportunity or not, is a different matter) and others a shaky foundation from which it is a challenge to build a productive life. Those who ask the poor why they can't pick themselves up and make a go of it in society are either ignorant of the impacts of poverty, or are willfully arming themselves with a rationale for condemnation.

Many have examined the impact of poverty on social indicators in the United States. The findings are disturbing. David Berliner (2013) tackles the relationship between poverty indicators and social well-being. Indicators include significant differences between wealthier homes and poor homes. Indicators include: Child Well-Being; Mental Health; Illegal Drug Use; Infant and Maternal Mortality; School Dropouts; Social Mobility; School Achievement; Teenage Birth Rate; and Rates of Imprisonment. Similarly, Ruby Payne (2013) cites the following indictors: instability of housing; violence; food insecurity; unemployment/underemployment; unaddressed health issues; frequent exposure to addiction; predators (both inside and outside the group); periodic homelessness; crowded housing/lack of personal space; incarceration; lots of time at agencies getting assistance; uneducated/undereducated adults; limited knowledge bases; and death.

In a University of South Africa (UNISA) presentation titled "Relationship between Education and Poverty" (Mbunyuza de Heer Menlah, 2010), similar findings were shared in the South African context. Characteristics of poverty in South Africa include: poor infrastructure – often few or no permanent roads; lack of piped water and sewage; lack of electricity; lack of access to telecommunications; high rates of unemployment and illiteracy; high mortality rates and health problems related to malnutrition; malaria; HIV and AIDS, and lack of access to medical facilities and medicine.

The UNISA presentation also cites the following related to school disparities. In poor households children often come to school hungry and unprepared to learn; most of the children who exit from poverty-area school systems have poor grades which make it difficult for them to access bursaries (scholarships) and other forms of financial assistance for university study; children often have no role models because of family and community deprivations; and there is a proliferation of child-headed families.

How do children fare during their first academic challenge – early grade reading? Spaull (2017) examined South African schools' success in this area. He cites data from the Progress in International Reading Literacy Study (PIRLS).[3] By the end of the third year of their formal education, children around the world are expected to read. Results from the most recent nationally-representative assessment of reading comprehension (PIRLS, 2016) show that 78% of Grade 4 learners in South Africa cannot read for meaning in any South African language (all 11 were assessed). It also revealed that South African learners had the lowest performance in reading comprehension across all 50 participating countries.

Experiences in the world provide background knowledge and emotional dispositions for the budding mind. As children grow, they bring with them the baggage of their environment. Some travel with a knapsack, others with a full-blown entourage of intellectual and psychological treasures.

"Cultural literacy," a term coined by E.D. Hirsch (1988), refers to the skill base necessary to achieve cultural capital. As such, a culturally literate person recognizes cultural cues, including language, narratives, idioms, historical references, popular culture trends, etc. Hirsch claims that literacy, i.e., the mechanics of reading and writing, while important, must be bolstered by a literacy regarding culture. At the juncture of both realms, a person will gain access to a sophisticated – and easily accessible – understanding of the world in which they live. Of course, children with little means have minimal access to the richness of cultural symbols and artifacts found in the wider world.

In "How to Get Your Mind to Read," Willingham (2017) examines knowledge as a provider of context. The more experiences a person has, the more readily available is understanding when reading. Much like Hirsch, Willingham believes that children who are learning to read in school face an uphill climb when they come from backgrounds that have offered them little experience beyond their home. Conversely, those from more fortunate backgrounds often come with experience to spare. Wealthier families in both the United States and South Africa are much more likely to provide a deeper and broader world of experiences for their children. A child from a wealthy family may have visited several countries by the time he or she enters school. A child from an impoverished family may have never gone farther than neighborhood streets by school age.

The law enforcement environment in a community can be freighted with bias that has a chilling effect on future chances for success for some. Numerous studies in the US have been conducted on the relationship between minority and majority rates of arrest, imprisonment, and death penalty punishment. One *Newsday* study (Maier & Choi, 2017) found that non-Whites were nearly five times as likely to be arrested on "stop and frisk" encounters with the police, this from an examination of police and court records from 2005–2016. Low-level crimes can lead to jail time and a criminal record which can diminish life chances, e.g., job opportunities. A similar study (Maier & Choi, 2017) found that Whites during the 2005–2016 period were far more likely to receive lighter sentences than minorities for possession of drugs. Results show that White, middle class offenders were more likely to afford legal counsel and receive lighter sentences, in some cases the sentence being attendance at a drug treatment center, than those who cannot afford counsel and end up in prison.

South Africa, post-apartheid, puts a twist on the law enforcement bias found in the US. Violence once directed by the apartheid police at Blacks is now directed at the poor, with Blacks still making up an overwhelming percentage of the poor. Police typically use more force in poor Black communities, and show more restraint in areas populated by Whites and wealthier Blacks. Where there is money, people have access to lawyers and therefore can defend themselves against unwarranted and excessive police engagement. Some critics go further.

> If police officers were once the agents of state repression under apartheid, they are now defenders of a status quo dominated by White business and a Black elite connected to an increasingly corrupt African National Congress. (Onishi, 2016, p. 6)

Still, other US studies have found unalloyed bias against people of color in everyday interactions and negotiations. Job applicants, whose names would be stereotypically regarded as "Black" names, were included in responses to a job application search with otherwise identical resumes to those with "White" names. "White" name applicants were 50% more likely to get a call back. Another study sent actual people to live interviews for low wage jobs. They were given identical resumes and the same interview training. The finding here was that African Americans with no criminal records were offered jobs at a rate as low as White applicants with criminal records. Similar bias was found in studies of medical procedure recommendations, car purchase price offerings, house sales, and apartment rental opportunities (see "steering" in chapter five), legislator response rates to constituents, and reply rates to inquiries for research opportunities at universities (Mullainathan, 2015).

Breaches of democratic justice are legion in voter rights in the US. The right to vote – and therefore the right to a degree of self-determination – has been curtailed or sabotaged since the 15th amendment (1870) barred states from a race-based denial of the franchise. One hundred fifty years later, the tactic of gerrymandering, the dividing of a region into voting districts so one political party will benefit, has become the new tool for nullifying Black voter rights. The message here seems to be: "Pick yourself up by your own bootstraps, even though we made sure the straps are out of reach."

3   School as the Great Leveler, Except When It's Not

In a radio panel discussion on the subject of school integration … one of the panelists appealed to South Africans to stop believing that 'education can carry the entire burden of transformation' (Alexander, 2004).

In the face of the distortions wrought by privilege in the community, it would seem plausible – and likely – that schools would come to the rescue of the disenfranchised. In fact, schools could provide the engines of fundamental change to bridge the divide. However, despite the best attempts by some, schools remain a part of the problem. Sadly, schools often showcase inequities. In a profoundly disturbing irony, those who have a predilection for scolding find varying school conditions and achievement disparities easy targets to boost their case.

A study of economic segregation in the United States, "How Entitled Parents Hurt Schools" (Lareau, Weininger, & Cox, 2018), revealed what the authors call "opportunity hoarding," in which well-to-do parents strategically work the system to assure that their children are in schools with the best resources. For example, when a region faces a challenge of redrawing boundaries to balance attendance, the powerful and privileged in the community marshal the support of influential players – pediatricians, public relations specialists, psychologists, urban planners, etc. – to steer the reassignment process to benefit their children. These parents have skillful organizational abilities, collecting data and crafting arguments to support their positions. Certainly, the skills of the upper middle class, used for boundaries arguments, are readily available when other challenges arise, e.g., securing their children a place in "gifted programs," even though they may not be recommended for them by school staff because these students do not exhibit the potential to succeed in such programs. I had such a circumstance to address when I first became a junior high school principal.

The faculty encouraged me to address the fact that there was an inordinate number of students in grade 9 who were enrolled in the gifted program. After a review of student academic achievement and teacher recommendation, it was clear that parental pressure had won the day – for years. I made the decision to reduce the number for the next year and heard a chorus of loud complaints from parents who were expecting special treatment. Individual parents petitioned me – implored me – to reconsider their child's placement, even though the child was clearly not eligible based on the criteria for entrance. They went so far as to petition my superiors, who, thankfully, supported my position.

In South African schools, apartheid seems mostly in place as it was before 1994. A *Cape Argus* news story (2019) highlights the findings of an Amnesty International study which warns that the legacy of apartheid will be fulfilled if the government does not address the needs of poor schools. Executive Director of Amnesty International South Africa, Shenilla Mohamed, commented on the matter:

> More than two decades after the end of apartheid, South Africa's education system still mirrors the apartheid years, with many schools serving

our poorest communities relying on outdated and poorly maintained infrastructure and a dire lack of teaching resources that provides a wholly inadequate learning space for young people. (*Cape Argus*, 2019)

The report cites alarming statistics: 78% of South Africa's 10-year-old learners cannot read; 61% of 11-year-olds cannot do basic mathematics, and; each year half of the 1.2 million children who were enrolled in grade 1 drop out by grade 12. Most distressing, the report discloses that 17% of the country's schools only provide dangerous pit latrines, leading to several deaths by drowning (*Cape Argus*, 2019).

The ANC brand, championed by no less than Mandela, has become anathema to many South African Blacks, especially with regard to education, with Gebrekidan and Onishi (2018) suggesting that "... the nation's poor schools are perhaps the ANC's greatest betrayal of the dream of Black South Africans." The fallout from this corruption is keenly visible in poor schools in townships. Corruption is rife in all segments of the educational system, depleting funds that would otherwise be used to improve school infrastructure.

In South Africa, I have traveled to many quintile one schools which serve the poorest communities. The experience is quite unnerving; the stark contrast between these no fee schools and the quintile five schools is most evident in the student/teacher ratio. In township schools, I have observed elementary school classrooms with 60 children sitting shoulder to shoulder in a room designed for half the number of learners. A principal shared with me that when he was told a class of 60 had to be increased the following year – to a class of 75 – he shuddered. It was only after the principal threatened to quit if the additional students were added that school authorities backed off.

3.1   *The 'Achievement Gap' Cudgel*

Creating and sustaining an even playing field for school students is the purported goal of both South Africa and the United States. However, students relegated to the untended portions of the field are still expected to perform like those living in parts which receive constant attention. The public is ready to pounce on the poor performers – Why can't they succeed like the rest of us? – an instinct fueled by nefarious messages from the authorities.

In a regular reminder to the public, schools across both South Africa and the United States post or announce test score results for public school students. School test data are periodically listed in newspaper columns for easier comparison from one region to the next. It comes as no surprise that schools with lower socio-economic status produce scores that are significantly lower than their wealthier counterparts. This publication ritual lends ammunition to those who are eager to criticize schools in poverty-stricken areas as predictably underperforming. Of course, the achievement gap antecedents, e.g., large class size, unsafe schools and communities, low expectations for student achievement, lack of rigor in the curriculum, access to health and social services, etc. (Gregg, 2019) are not in play during the discourse. As Kirp (2012) reminds us:

> Amid the ceaseless and cacophonous debates about how to close the achievement gap, we've turned away from one tool that has been shown to work: school desegregation. That strategy, ushered in by the landmark 1954 Supreme Court decision in Brown v. Board of Education, has been unceremoniously ushered out, an artifact in the museum of failed social experiments.

Kirkland (2010) makes the case that the achievement gap construct normalizes Whiteness. He suggests that it has become weaponized – a "blunt force" to obscure past and present racial oppression. He cites Fanon, who as early as 1952 suggested "… the fact of the juxtaposition of the White and Black races has created a massive psycho-existential complex" (as cited in Kirkland, 2010). Kirkland continues: "… the constant and continuous comparison of students of color (African and otherwise) to White students as buffered by test scores reinforces … differences in the extreme" (Kirkland, 2010).

The current iteration of standardized testing has a racist pedigree. During World War I, standardized test results steered 1.5 million soldiers to units segregated by race and test scores. The tests were considered deeply biased. Army testing during this period was the catalyst for standardized testing regimes to expand in public schools. During the 1920s, an aptitude test was considered an important part of the college admissions process since at the time intelligence and ethnic origin were considered connected. "The results of such a test could be used to limit admissions of particularly undesirable ethnicities" (Rosales, n.d.). In the 1930s, multiple choice tests were an integral part of the testing culture in schools as well as the Harvard-adopted aptitude testing (the SAT) to choose scholarship recipients. In the 1950s and 60s universities in the United States were searching for the best and the brightest students and standardized test results became a pivotal criterion. This did not bode well for students of color since the tests were widely regarded as biased. Enrollments in colleges at that time experienced a huge racial gap. Some would argue that today we are more test obsessed/achievement gap focused than ever before. Starting with international tests which compare national achievement scores, down to third graders who suffer standardized assessments as a national mandate, there exists a "reification and ranking" mentality (Gould, 1981) which performs a regular testing surgery on the body politic which separates those who can from those who can't.

In South Africa, there has been a long list of testing programs post-apartheid (examples include: the verification tests; Common Task Assessment tests; Annual National Assessment tests) which publicly display deficiencies by number-crunching. Private school learners take a "matric" exam before graduating from secondary school to determine if they are eligible for tertiary education. These learners have "... inched closer to the magical 100% pass rate following a stellar performance from the class of 2018 ..." (Koko, 2019). The pass rate was 98.92%. for 2018 and 98.76% for 2017. Public school students take a different matric exam. The passing rate in these schools, not surprisingly, is largely correlated along racial and economic lines.

In both countries, there is an unspoken truth about the testing emphases. Political appointees like the Basic Education Minister in South Africa and the Secretary of Education in the United States are likely to share the results of large scale testing with the public, a practice which is mimicked by more local representatives. While those in the political class praise the schools which do well, they take to task schools that don't. This test-shaming is another way to laud the accomplishments of the privileged while looking down upon the meager results of the others. This handy device for keeping the elite satisfied, has been used for years in both countries.

Despite the recurring theme of test-score announcements applauding well-to-do communities, many have denounced what some have called "weapons of mass instruction." Pointed criticisms of the emphasis on tests have been circulating for many years in both the US and South Africa. In an article in *The Times* – with offices in Cape Town and Durban – the experts agreed:

> ... teaching has become test-coaching time in many classrooms .... The testing and monitoring culture can make the learning environment toxic because there is just too much stress all round ... some teachers are just preparing pupils to pass the test instead of covering the curriculum. (Child, 2013)

These very same criticisms are leveled by teachers and parents in the US, where standardized tests have been mandated in grades 3–8 throughout the country since the inception of No Child Left Behind, a federal program inaugurated in 2001. Some parents have chosen to "opt-out" of the tests, believing that the stress and competition of the testing regimes are undermining their children's growth.

3.2   The "Victory Lap" Ruse
Compounding the public ignominy of those who are "not trying" is the "we're winning" gambit. Politicians, needing to demonstrate they are tackling the

problems of the poor, especially poor schoolchildren, are eager to share school results, even if their announcements are exaggerated and, sometimes, outright lies. This feature of the portrait only serves to confuse the issue, perhaps the goal of the keepers of the status quo.

Declaring victory over educational achievement disparities has become a common thrust of remarks from politicians and others in the ministerial ranks in both the US and South Africa. They have, in most cases, taken test data information and fit it conveniently into the narrative that things are improving, in some cases, hyperbolically invoking the change as a "miracle." The unabashed canard has a dual purpose. First, it offers a self-congratulatory high five to those in charge. Second, it supplies a free pass to those very same people, absolving them of more sincere, albeit tough and unpopular, approaches.

Child (2018) reports that Angie Motshekga, the Minister of Basic Education in South Africa, declared that poor schools were doing better than wealthier schools in the province of the Free State, but she ignored the increasing number of high school and university drop-outs in the calculation. (One reason that some schools had a higher matric result was the large number of students who dropped out before grade 10.) In fact, the touted matric pass rate of 86% would drop to 36% if the dropouts were included.

Motshekga applauded the increase from 26% to 28.7% of bachelor passes, which allow pupils to apply for university. What she left out was that only about two thirds who qualify for university actually attend, this according to her department's own report. She also did not explain why 629,155 students started matric and 534,484 actually wrote the matric exam (passage of which is required for a "school-leaving" certificate) which represented a drop-out rate of 15% last year.

Motshekga engaged in other sketchy arithmetic in order to claim a win for her department. She lauded the results of no-fee schools (those which serve communities whose residents cannot afford tuition costs on their own) which she claimed had better bachelor passes than fee schools. She trumpeted the finding that for every one fee-paying school, where 80% to 100% of the students passed, there were two no-fee schools with the same result. What she conveniently omitted was that no-fee schools outnumber fee-paying schools by four to one. According to the National Exam report, there are actually 4,929 no-fee schools and 1,317 fee-paying schools.

Johnathan Jansen, former University of Free State vice-chancellor, took Motshekga to task on Facebook: "Dear South Africans, why are we so gullible? Here goes Minister Angie Motshekga once again leading you by the nose."

In the United States a similar stretch of the facts has been outed by those taking a closer look. Weiss (2014) in her report, "Stop Counting on Education

Miracles/Policymakers who proclaim miraculous progress in education don't usually have their facts straight," shines a light on famous – and false – declarations of achievement by well-known politicians. The list is distressing, especially because it is not surprising.

– George W. Bush, as he campaigned for President in 2000, and was the sitting governor of Texas, touted the "Texas Miracle" which saw gains in standardized test scores after the state put in place new accountability measures. In fact, Texas had made gains no larger than most other states, through data that did not count certain students and other enrollment irregularities. In fact, almost 20 years later, test scores and graduation rates of minority students continue to be extremely low.
– In 2011, in New York City, Mayor Michael Bloomberg proclaimed that the achievement gap between Black and Latino students and White and Asian kids was cut in half during his administration. A closer look showed that when the gap was rounded to the nearest whole number there was not any change since 2003.
– In Chicago, Urban Prep had the distinction of graduating 100% of its students. The asterisk here reveals that half of the students dropped out between freshman and senior year – those who couldn't graduate – to achieve their "perfect" rate.
– In perhaps the most egregious lie, the former Secretary of Education, Arne Duncan, made the obscene statement about how a devastating hurricane that pummeled New Orleans was "the best thing that happened to the education system in New Orleans." He based his claim on data from Tulane University Cowen Institute citing the "miraculous" gains in the Recovery School District, designed, post-Katrina, as an all-charter district. After scrutiny of the Cowen report, it was found that its methodology was flawed and its conclusions inaccurate. A full retraction was issued. In fact, the district's student achievement data were unremarkable, even substantially below comparison groups in some cases.

The truth? Sorry, doesn't serve our purpose right now. Maybe at a later date.

Notes

1   Thurgood Marshall was the first African-American to serve on the Supreme Court. Prior to his service as Associate Justice he argued several cases before the Supreme Court, including *Brown v. Board of Education.*

2 While Moynihan did not coin the phrase, "culture of poverty" – anthropologist Oscar
   Lewis did – the sentiment became part of popular folklore. "The description of the
   urban Black family as caught in an inescapable 'tangle of pathology' of unmarried
   mothers and welfare dependency was seen as attributing self-perpetuating moral
   deficiencies to Black people, as if blaming them for their own misfortune" (Cohen,
   2010).

3 PIRLS was inaugurated in 2001 and is conducted every 5 years by the International
   Association for the Evaluation of Educational Achievement (IEA). Fifty countries
   were represented in the 2016 administration. Jurisdictions use the comparative data
   to inform policy.

CHAPTER 7

The Sanctimony of Noblesse Oblige

> No doubt, unity is something to be desired, to be striven for, but it cannot
> be willed by mere declarations.
>
> THEODORE BIKEL, Actor, Musician, Political Activist (1924–2015)

∴

Surely, many who are wealthy, or who otherwise occupy stations of power and
privilege within a society, are benefactors of the needy and supporters – in
some cases champions – of righteous causes.

Does this altruism come with a caveat?

It may seem cynical to suspect motives of the generous, but without some
skepticism, the structural racism that undergirds everyday events and interactions may never be dismantled. Is there an agenda freighted with self-interest
when overtures are made to the less fortunate? Do we bask in the Klieg lights
when we are feted for a good deed? What about hypocrisy? Do we say one
thing and mean another or do we use the language of giving to give us cover
for a misdeed?

Do we walk away after our charity event, feeling relieved that we have contributed to the cause? Our guilt reduced, if not extinguished altogether. Nothing more to do right now. And, what about those who have a vested interest in
the status quo? Will they erect Potemkin Villages that will drown out the noise
of racial marginalization?

1 "Double Consciousness"

Those who are fortunate enough to enter the resource sweepstakes with a
legacy of privilege, therefore enjoying the best housing situations and educational opportunities for their children, are quite often vocal about the need
for equity amongst all racial/ethnic groups. In her study of five disparate Long
Island school districts, Wells (2009) cites survey data which demonstrate that
residents of all backgrounds in the region believe that something should be
done to break down barriers between communities. However, those with the

© KONINKLIJKE BRILL NV, LEIDEN, 2020 | DOI: 10.1163/9789004444430_007

most power and privilege – typically the White communities – are stubbornly fortifying their boundaries against interlopers while at the same time decrying segregation. Wells calls this phenomenon, a form of "double consciousness." She also references Myrdal (1946), whose book *The American Dilemma* makes the case that White Americans are caught up in a vicious cycle, in which they oppress Negroes and then denigrate them for their poor performance, all the while firmly standing by the trope that all men are created equal. (Note that Myrdal wrote about the issue nearly 75 years ago, but the sentiment could have been posted in an Op-Ed piece in today's newspaper.)

In South Africa, after 1994, the power structure shifted from rich White people in charge to rich White people and rich Black people in charge. As mentioned in Chapter Two, this transition profoundly disrupted the proposition that after apartheid was dismantled, all would benefit, especially those most victimized by past regimes. Instead, a "double consciousness" emerged in the upper echelons of the Black community as they moved into spaces in society formerly reserved for Whites only, spaces which afforded them power and opportunity. At the same time, they decry the abuses of apartheid. This, while the vast majority of Black people continue to suffer from a lack of fundamental resources, in living conditions that are deplorable by any standard. Those experiencing (practicing?) double consciousness are remarkably immune to the psychological pathology known as cognitive dissonance. Somehow, they have made peace with themselves – charitably giving as they do, but supporting structural frameworks that continue to divide.

The presentation of homilies by those who have purported liberal dispositions are the tools of distraction. Dog whistles (which include coded words and racially-tinged memes) are the communication devices used by those who are compelled to share their intolerance under cover, lest they be called out as racist. And, there is the altogether disingenuous gambit when those who try to hide their bias do so with an aggressively heartfelt demand for social justice. A Black mother living in a White St. Louis community feels that her family is safe and the environment is pleasant, but in both her job and her life, she says racial bias is still evident. "Discrimination is different today ... It's with a smile. It's with a pleasant voice" (Eligon, 2015, p. 1)

Another forlorn example of the double-consciousness effect resides in the self-appointed racial divide scholar/missionary. Here is where self-reflection is both important to my work and painful to my soul.

My positionality as a privileged White male university professor researching a book about the racial divide is fraught with a callousness I cannot overlook. Through my work, I believe that I am exposing a social malady found in South Africa and the United States. My work is particularly rewarding when I take "field trips" through townships to gather data. I feel as if I am examining a species in a laboratory, poring over the hydra, trying to discover why every time we cut off its head, two more grow back. At the end of the workday, I go out to celebrate a job well done at an exclusive winery in the Western Cape. When I return to the States, my conscience eased, I go back to my (virtually) all White college faculty – truly the "ivory" tower, folks – and present my findings. Afterwards, I return to my (literally) all White neighborhood. I pronounce myself a champion of the oppressed and hope that others will give me a shout out. My good work will precede me. I am untouchable. My virtue is unimpeachable. I am a crusader for justice. I am from the liberal Northeast, where we practice, as Jordan Peele says, "self-congratulatory tolerance" (Morris, 2017).

I am most definitely not a racist. Although …

I had a hard time squaring my high-mindedness with a discussion I had with a taxi driver in a 2014 trip to Johannesburg. Nelson Mandela had died in 2013 and I asked how things were going after this milestone event. His perspective was that things have gotten better. "People just live with each other now."

My journal comments for that exchange read: "I was disappointed to hear this because I want more work to do, i.e., if things get better I won't have the racist paradigm to explore and play with." In my more sober moments, however, I reflect on the seriousness of the work. Social justice scholarship, at its best, constructs a message that must be delivered so that the public can recognize it and act upon it. Scholarship on its own is both arrogant and impotent in the face of social injustice.

2   The Enchantment of "Giving"

… it was always advisable to examine carefully any gifts borne by the ruling class of the United States of America. (Alexander, 2004)[1]

Dinner Guest: Me

I know I am
The Negro Problem
Being wined and dined,
Answering the usual questions
That come to white mind
Which seeks demurely
To probe in polite way

The why and wherewithal
Of darkness U.S.A. –
Wondering how things got this way
In current democratic night,
Murmuring gently
Over fraises du bois,

"I'm so ashamed of being white."

The lobster is delicious,
The wine divine,
And center of attention
At the damask table, mine.
To be a Problem on
Park Avenue at eight
Is not so bad.
Solutions to the Problem,
Of course, wait.
(Langston Hughes)

As Hughes suggests, the White, rich and powerful have become skilled at staging events which invite conversation about race and poverty. But an event's goal turns out to be a mirage when the discussion does not earnestly deal with the problem, i.e., the event is pure theater. Eusebius McKaiser, a South African political analyst, broadcaster and public speaker, suggests that if you are a White person who leaves out your own "agency" in the problems associated with racism, then you should "switch off the news for a little while and enjoy your glass of wine on your balcony in the suburbs feeling above the fray" (McKaiser, 2015).

Those who underwrite initiatives to support communities of color are often applauded by the larger society for their good work. In some cases, they are lionized as saviors of the needy. There are congratulations all around. These people do good work for sure. However, sometimes the most laudable initiatives should be examined for parts unknown.

The ingratitude that comes from critics of those who give seems appalling. Nevertheless, if we are serious about examining all the operant conditions that continue racial and economic divides, all behaviors are open for inspection. My experience sometimes offers me a window into this phenomenon.

I was invited to a lecture given by the distinguished educational leader, Geoffrey Canada, whose extraordinary accomplishment of engineering the development and longevity of the Harlem Children's Zone, a charter school in Harlem, New York, is widely acclaimed. At one point in the lecture he shared an experience he has repeatedly. When talking to an audience of White folks and asking them if they had aspirations for their children to go to college, almost every hand goes up. Not so when he is talking to an audience of Black people. He asks: Why is this so? His message was simple: We need to include expectations from all communities in our consideration of unequal outcomes. The rest of his remarks were equally impressive.

While Canada's accomplishments are significant, there is a catch related to the source of dollars that fund the work, a point made by his detractors. He emphasizes public/corporate donor dollars to fund the schools. He has come under fire for messaging that it is the corporate sector that comes to the rescue of poor Black kids, when, in fact, many suggest that it is that very same sector that created the circumstances that the poor live under (Kim, 2016). This conundrum should not dismiss the good work done by the HCZ on behalf of disenfranchised school children. However, we cannot, and should not, be ignorant of forces at work in the larger society that capture the public imagination by calling for a rebalancing of the economic landscape, and, at the same time, perpetuate the status quo.

3   Polite Fiction

In what may be the most famous American novel ever published, *To Kill a Mockingbird* by Harper Lee (1962), the reader is offered plenty to think about regarding race. Lee tackles the harsh realities of the 1930s South when Blacks were second class citizens with virtually no civic protections. Atticus Finch, an attorney – and a stalwart member of the community – takes on the case of a Black man, Tom Robinson, who is falsely accused of raping a White woman. His legal skills are on display as he skillfully uncovers a scheme to frame Tom. His final summation is breathtakingly courageous, frank and damning, all the more so because both the jury and the packed courtroom are filled with his neighbors, including his young son and daughter. He cites the White communities' "... cynical assumption – the evil assumption – that all Negroes lie, that all Negroes are basically immoral beings, that all Negro men are not to be trusted around our women ..." All this to no avail as the jury finds the defendant guilty as charged.

At one point during the course of the trial, we learn – through Atticus' children – that he has been arguing with his sister. Scout shares what she has heard with her brother Jem: "She won't let him alone about Tom Robinson. She almost said Atticus was disgracin' the family." His response: "... [I'm] in favor of Southern womanhood as much as anybody, but not for preserving polite fiction at the expense of human life" (Lee, 1962).

How many of us are guilty of employing "polite fiction" responses when issues of racism arise? While these responses may not rise to the level of court-room drama, they nevertheless contribute to a disingenuous social discourse, beneath which may be a boiling pot of intense – and confounding – reactions. Are we especially sensitive to racially-tinged remarks, insisting that they are inappropriate? Even if we harbor resentments, fears and disdain for a particu-lar person or group, would we ever deign to share those? Are we frightened by a response from family, friends, and colleagues that may call us out as racist? In what is perhaps an odd and unexpected question in the imbroglio of racial tension, are we hiding viewpoints that we fear will be challenged and some-how undermine our self-perceptions as a non-racist? Confusing though it may seem, the possibility this fear is real may be worth examining. And, in a bizarre iteration of keeping things "nice," are we, at times, critical of people of color, not because we believe in the criticism, but because we can better fit in to pop-ular notions, thereby avoiding public controversy.

Galman, Pica-Smith, and Rosenberger (2010) in "Aggressive and Tender Navigations: Educators Confront Whiteness in Their Practice," address the issue of confronting the truth about our own prejudices, especially those of educators. They found, in part, that teachers can fail students of color, "in the name of being nice by privileging White comfort to avoid bringing conflict to the fore ..." (p. 233). What they refer to as "economies of niceness" were used as currency during classroom discussions to be "traded" as place holders to avoid more critical themes. "In short, niceness filled up discourse that could have been allotted to race talk" (Galman, Pica-Smith, & Rosenberger, 2010, p. 233). Another distinct feature of this classroom milieu was that anyone who did open up with a brave comment condemning racism was considered a trou-blemaker. Researchers also found that "sanitizing" racial language helped to sustain a level of comfort during classroom discussions.

My self-reflections in this regard have been unnerving at times. I strive to unpack the truth about racial tensions and consider myself an agent of change. However, I must admit that I have been guilty many times of avoid-ing honest talk about race in my own classrooms, whether I was teaching in K-12 classrooms or college programs. In what is clearly a contradiction in my stated approach/goal for honest interchange about a difficult subject, I shrink from navigating the inevitable contests that will ensue among my students if

I encourage them to strip off the veneer and get to the bottom of the anger, rage, confusion, and mystery of the racial divide. I prefer a politeness around the topic.

I am trying to overcome my fear of confrontation, although it's not an easy assignment.

Lately, when I begin meetings at the university on the racial divide with my colleagues – or in other professional settings – I start with this message: "We need to be honest in our discussion. It will not be business as usual. If, at the end of the conversation, you feel comfortable, then we have not learned much."

4   "Poverty Porn" – "Ghetto Tourism"

A White, middle-class, South African family experiment grabbed the attention of the world press. The Hewitt family, which included two toddlers, decided to leave their gated community in Pretoria for a month to see what living in a township would be like. They traded a lifestyle of comfort for one of deprivation to see how township neighbors lived. (Their home in suburban Pretoria was just six miles away from Phomolong, a densely populated shantytown in Mamelodi.) They were roundly criticized by some, bewildering to others, and supported for their venture as well. One commentator, Busi Dlamini, executive director at the time of rights group Dignity International, honored the noble motives of the family, while at the same time labeling their adventure "poverty porn." The Hewitts' experiences taught them much about township daily living. They made friends while they were there and planned to continue these relationships (Polgreen, 2013).

Like the Hewitts, I am intrigued by abject poverty. I have been, what one might call, a socio-political-poverty travel agent as I have conducted tours of South African townships for my colleagues from the United States. One occasion, when I was touring on my own, is indicative of my experience – including the self-recriminations. Below is an excerpt from a journal entry after a visit to the Kayamundi township in October 2014.

> I walked into a shack in the Kayamundi township and asked if I could speak with the people inside for a minute or two. There were six adults in a two-room shack that I estimated was about 300 square feet. I introduced myself. No one seemed to mind that I was in their home. I told them, amongst other things, that I enjoy the energy and enthusiasm of the children in South Africa. They all agreed that the children are spirited and friendly. It was

quite shocking to see what small quarters people live in and, also, how, in the middle of a work day, six adults were sitting around just talking. After-wards, for quite some time, I had this nagging self-loathing. I had been an unrepentant voyeur in my visit. I considered the people I talked to as objects in an exhibition, there to satisfy my intellectual curiosities about race and class. I especially felt that way when I thought about the loads of photos I had taken of street scenes in their neighborhood.

Jonathan Turton (2017) addresses society-sanctioned voyeurism in a piece called "Ghetto Tourism." It is interesting to read his opening paragraph in light of the current project.

Upon hearing the word safari you'll most likely picture the green, rolling hills of Africa or at the very least, an ill-fitting pair of khaki shorts. But what if I were to tell you a different kind of safari exists? One that takes place in Bushwick – one of New York's most impoverished, if notoriously hip, areas? (Turton, 2017)

Turton shares his experience of joining a walking tour through a predomi-nately Black neighborhood in Brooklyn, New York. The "tourists" were mostly well-to-do White people who were being led by another well-to-do White per-son. People who live in the neighborhood have, for decades, lived in difficult circumstances. At the time the article was written, 30% of residents in the area lived below the poverty line. And, in a 2015 report, the unemployment rate was the second highest in Brooklyn. A local citizen saw the irony in the situation: The visitors felt safe when they were walking around the area with another White person; otherwise they were afraid to enter the neighborhood. The Bushwick community has been on the receiving end of much misfortune. It became less stable economically after World War II. The neighborhood was assaulted by looters and arsonists during a NYC blackout in 1977. Damage was estimated to be $300,000,000 as 35 blocks were trashed. A third of the busi-nesses closed down. Drug and social problems skyrocketed.

The tourists are looking for "a fix of inner-city realism" according to Tur-ton. The ostensible reason for the tour is to observe street art, graffiti that is painted on shutters and factory sides. Of course, the art focus is interrupted by other visuals, including a car that passes by, a passenger shouting, "Don't listen to him, he's a liar." The tour passes a rehab center for violent criminals. The homes that are passed on the tour are filled with problems, including inad-equate heating, plumbing breakdowns, cracks and holes, mice and rats, etc. The tour offers a bizarre kaleidoscope of contrasting images – from art work to heartbreak. As Turton opines: "People live in Bushwick. It's not a nature reserve or museum." And, in what may be the most important observation, he asks:

> ... how would [the tourists] feel about Bushwick residents walking around their neighbourhood three times a week, pointing and taking photographs of their homes, local businesses and streets? Would it be okay to congregate as they do, in a Connecticut suburb? (Turton, 2017)

5   Celebration Fatigue in the US

> You're going to relegate my history to a month? I don't want a Black history month. Black history is American history. (Morgan Freeman, actor)

In a piece entitled, "So You Think You're an Anti-Racist?" Paul Gorski (2010) dives into the fray with a pungent perspective about the illusion of celebration as repair.

> Food fairs, multicultural festivals, and dialogue programs are fun and interesting events that may bring people together temporarily. But, do they eradicate, or even mitigate, racism? The most important, and seemingly most difficult, anti-racism shift for White people is to understand that confronting racism is going to be uncomfortable, difficult, emotional, and painful. Ultimately, racial conflict is only a symptom of systemic racism, and we never will stop racism with cultural programming. (Gorski, 2010)

Below is a partial list of festivals in the United States honoring African-American culture, taking place over a four month period, August–November, 2019. (The total number of events for the time period – as reported on the "everfest"[2] website – is 35.)
- Black Harvest Film Festival (Chicago, IL)
- Capital City Black Film Festival (Austin, TX)
- African Festival of the Arts (Chicago, IL)
- Stockton Black Family Day (Stockton, CA)
- African American Cultural Festival (Raleigh, NC)
- Black L.U.V. Festival (Washington, DC)
- Lexington Roots and Heritage Festival (Lexinton, KY)
- Urban World Film Festival (New York)
- Nashville African Street Festival (Nashville, TN)

- Miss Africa (Twin Falls, ID)
- Jubilee Festival of Black History and Culture (Columbia, SC)
- National Black Arts Festival (Atlanta, GA)
- Oakland Black Cowboy Parade (Oakland, CA)
- Black Expo South (Charleston, SC)
- AfroSolo Arts Festival (San Francisco, CA)
- National Black Book Festival, Houston, TX)

Sports, music, and other popular culture offerings provide a further platform to showcase African American accomplishments. Some of the most celebrated stars in these areas are people of color.

As a White person, I am aware that it may be arrogant and off-putting for me to stake out a position on the matter of Black celebrations, i.e., that there are too many of them and they have the effect of diverting attention from structural racism. And, I am also aware that there exist many other ethnicities, religious, and cultural groups that are regularly celebrated in the US. However, I am proposing that, at some society-sized, unconscious level, there exists a need for raucous support and cheering of Black causes and celebrations thus creating a "flashbang" effect to divert attention.

"Flashbang" is the term used by police when they create a diversion in a demonstration when the crowd, usually one gathered together to protest, gets dangerously uproarious. An explosive device is thrown away from the group so that they will switch their attention to the flash and away from the protest. Sometimes referred to as a stun grenade, the appliance is a non-lethal explosive, that produces a blinding flash, accompanied by a loud blast. A crowd literally becomes stunned by the sight and sound, redirecting the energy in the field. It works for the moment.

Is it going too far to say that public adoration of Black and Brown entertainers, athletes, and such, and regular festivals and holidays paying tribute to milestones and accomplishments of people of color are, in part, designed to divert attention from a racist ethos that is still prevalent in the US?

Perhaps. But the outsized attention to accomplishments of Black people and the celebrity accorded to certain people in that community – in light of the constancy and venality of structural racism – may be a topic ripe for further discussions.

Black History Month began as Negro History Week in 1926, a result of historian Carter G. Woodson's initiative to highlight accomplishments of African Americans, whom he believed, should be included in the American history pantheon (Vox, 2019). Woodson began lobbying for his cause when the racist film *The Birth of a Nation* was released. He helped found the Association for the Study of Negro Life and History which published the periodical, *The Journal of*

Negro History. African Americans were quick to support Negro History week and over the coming decades the project remained alive, albeit in the background of the American social and political scenery.

During the 1960s Civil Rights movement, the dedication to honoring African Americans was energized. In 1976, the occasion of the American bi-centennial, Negro History Week became Black History Month and US President Gerald R. Ford urged Americans to celebrate. President Jimmy Carter officially recognized Black History Month and, with the federal government endorsement, regular events and celebrations took place across the country, especially in schools. As the 21st Century rolled in, heralding the election of the first African-American President, there were those who questioned the meaning of Black History Month. Commentator Byron Williams suggested that Black History Month had become "trite, stale, and pedestrian rather than informative and thought-provoking" and served only to relegate "the achievements of African Americans to an adjunct status in American history" (Vox, 2019).

6   Co-Opting Madiba/South Africa's Potemkin Village

As mentioned in an earlier chapter, the Sandton Mall in Sandton – located in the Johannesburg municipality – is one of the most beautiful shopping centers in the world. I have visited the site twice in my travels. Upscale in every way, the mall is the perfect well-to-do consumer retreat. Classy restaurants and interior hallways lined with expensive stores greet each other at intersections. The mall centerpiece (which I referred to previously) is a giant statue of Nelson Mandela. In the grand outdoor arena – which provides entrance ways into the mall proper – stands the statue, 6 meters (20 ft) high and 2.3 meters (7 ft 7 in) from elbow to elbow. The statue weighs in at 2.5 tons. It has been described as "towering," "imposing," and a "focal point" for the entire area.

The height of the surrounding shops is five to six stories. Every hundred feet or so on the walls of these buildings – visible everywhere from the outside of the mall – there is a two to three story photo of Mandela, accompanied by one of his famous quotes – in his handwriting! It seems that the country's financial czars and planners know all too well that if they want to make money, they should invoke the name and spirit of Mandela. One poster at the main entranceway suggests:

Find the Madiba in You

Others include:

If we unite and respect diversity, we will become one nation

For to be free is not only to cast off ones chains, but to live in a way that respects and enhances the freedom of others.

The sun shall never set on such a glorious achievement as freedom. Let freedom reign

Sometimes it falls on a generation to be great. You can be that great generation.

Let your greatness blossom.

Some would argue that there is no contradiction here. There is nothing but the display of prosperity that reflects the new South Africa, the one that Mandela fought for. But, tens of millions of South Africans, whose means do not even cover the costs of running water and food for their families, are precluded from enjoying the fruits of this change, a new apartheid, if you will. In this new divide, as noted earlier, wealthy and powerful Black people are welcome to shop and eat and revel in their new-found freedoms. The White and Black people who are fortunate enough to be on the winning side of the divide, exclaim that all are invited to participate in the new South African life buffet.

Just make sure you bring plenty of cash. Major credit cards will be accepted as well.

Notes

1 Alexander (2004) on the South African Bantu Act, which was modeled after *Brown v. BOE.*
2 Details regarding festivals of all types can be found at https://www.everfest.com/

No Brief Candle: The Dreams, Determination, and Wisdom of Nelson Mandela and Martin Luther King

... Out, out, brief candle!
Life's but a walking shadow, a poor player,
That struts and frets his hour upon the stage,
And then is heard no more ...

WILLIAM SHAKESPEARE, *Macbeth*

∙∙∙

Life is no 'brief candle' to me. It is sort of a splendid torch which I have a hold of for the moment, and I want to make it burn as brightly as possible before handing it over to future generations.

GEORGE BERNARD SHAW

∙∙
∙

Nelson Mandela and Martin Luther King were agents with a message from the same source. They used their outsize bully pulpit to trouble the status quo in their respective countries. They insisted that the powerful and the privileged bear witness to a movement determined to change the course of history. No more would skin color differences translate into opportunity differences. And, those who had been damaged by this paradigm in the past would be welcomed into a new order where all are equal and regarded with respect.

Although they lived 7,000 miles and an ocean apart, and Mandela was born 12 years before King, but outlived him by 44 years, they had much in common. They achieved worldwide recognition, both winning the Nobel Peace Prize and garnering accolades for their work wherever they traveled. They were also vilified by prominent figures who saw them as a threat to established (White) power and order. Their boldness in the fight against social injustice, their high profile call for freedom, and their ability to rouse the multitudes cast them as characters that had to be taken out, one way or the other. King was assassinated

© KONINKLIJKE BRILL NV, LEIDEN, 2020 | DOI: 10.1163/9789004444430_008

at age 39. Mandela spent 27 years in prison. The threat was over in one case and caged in the other. Turns out that was wishful thinking for those who feared these giants of social justice.

1   46664

Rolihlahla Mandela was born into the Madiba clan in the Eastern Cape, on July 18,1918. He was given the Christian name "Nelson" by his primary school teacher – as was the custom. He went on to secondary school and then began studying for a BA at the University College of Fort Hare. He did not complete the degree. He was expelled for joining a student protest. Mandela worked as a mine security officer for a time and then went on to complete his BA at the University of South Africa (UNISA). Afterwards, he obtained a two-year diploma in law which allowed him to practice law and, in 1952, he established – with Oliver Tambo – the first Black law firm in South Africa.

For the rest of his life, Mandela was an active member and leader of numerous anti-apartheid initiatives. His life was devoted to the cause of freedom. As such, he sacrificed his own freedom many times, being detained or imprisoned by a ruling White class fearful of his devotion to overthrowing their racialized version of governance.

His political involvement included membership in the ANC (African National Congress) where he helped organize the ANC Youth League, which would be the catalyst for a more aggressive campaign by the ANC at-large. He was chosen as the "National Volunteer-in-Chief" of the "Defiance Campaign," which used civil disobedience as a lever for change. He – along with 19 comrades – was sentenced under the Suppression of Communism Act, to nine months of hard labor, a sentence which was suspended for two years. He was arrested in 1956 and was the subject – along with many others – of what became known as the Treason Trial, which lasted for several years, ending in an acquittal for Mandela and 28 of the accused.

The Sharpeville massacre occurred in March of 1960. Police killed 69 unarmed people who were protesting the pass laws. This incident would become a defining moment in modern-day South African history. The ANC and the PAC (Pan Africanist Congress) were banned and Mandela and thousands of other people were detained during a state of emergency.

Mandela would be called upon over the next several years to occupy leadership positions in the struggle against apartheid, including the planning of a national strike. The strike was called off in light of a massive preparation of government security to counteract the effort. In 1961, Mandela was asked to head up an armed struggle and he helped to establish *Spear of the Nation* which was responsible for a series of explosions. In 1962, he secretly left the country to garner support from other nations for the struggle. Upon his return, he was charged with leaving the country without a permit and inciting workers to strike. He was sentenced to five years in prison, a term he began to serve at the Pretoria Local Prison. He was transferred to Robben Island prison in 1963. Mandela had become the target of a relentless pursuit by the apartheid government to curtail his participation in what was fast becoming an all-out rebellion. Mandela was assigned the number 46664 when he arrived at Robben Island prison in 1964. He was the 466th prisoner to arrive that year and his assigned number then became 46664.

In October of 1963, in what would become known as the Rivonia Trial, Mandela and 10 others were tried for sabotage. He faced the death penalty. Instead, he was given a life sentence. He spent the next 18 years in the Robben Island prison and then was transferred to Pollsmoor Prison in Cape Town where he was imprisoned for the next 7 years. He spent his last 14 months in confinement in a house in Paarl. He was released in February of 1990 just after the lifting of the ban on the ANC and the PAC. (It is noteworthy that in his time in prison he was offered at least three conditional releases and refused them all.)

Mandela's sacrifice for the greater good impacted him deeply with regard to his connections with his family. In prison, he was allowed brief visits from family members. When his mother was quite ill, she came to visit and was allowed a 45 minute rather than a 30 minute visit. His mother died shortly afterwards. Mandela, the eldest child and only son, shared his painful response to her passing.

> A mother's death causes a man to look back on and evaluate his own life. Her difficulties, her poverty, made me question once again whether I had taken the right path. That was always the conundrum: Had I made the right choice in putting the people's welfare even before that of my own family? For a long time, my mother had not understood my commitment to the struggle. My family had not asked for or even wanted to be involved in the struggle, but my involvement penalized them.
>
> But I came back to the same answer. In South Africa, it is hard for a man to ignore the needs of the people, even at the expense of his own family. I had made my choice, and in the end, she had supported it. But that did not lessen the sadness I felt at not being able to make her life more comfortable, or the pain of not being able to lay her to rest. (Mandela, 1994, p. 445)

In 1991 Mandela was elected ANC President and in 1993 he and South African President FW de Klerk jointly won the Nobel Peace Prize. In 1994 Mandela was voted in as President of South Africa in the first democratically held elections. He stepped down as President, true to his word, in 1999 after one term. (Many thought that he would remain President for life.) He continued his public service, working with the Nelson Mandela Children's Fund he set up in 1995 as well as establishing the Nelson Mandela Foundation and The Mandela Rhodes Foundation.

Nelson Mandela died on December 5, 2013, in his home in Johannesburg.

In 2013, I traveled to South Africa with a contingent of educators, a journey I had been making for several years. This time was different. Nelson Mandela died during our visit. My first thoughts were that the country would erupt into turmoil, the glue that held the social fabric together, i.e., Mandela, now being gone. Would people riot in the streets? Would they go after foreigners, especially White foreigners, now that their patriarch was not watching? I was afraid that Black people would harm me. I realized, sadly, that I was not above such an impulse.

Turns out, I was wrong in my assumptions. Not only was there no extreme social turmoil, the people were solemn and respectful, perhaps more respectful than usual. There were spontaneous eruptions of songs (on street corners) which were dedicated to Madiba. The conversations we had with all people were both emotional and reverential. They wanted to talk about Mandela and the role he played in their country's history. Far from losing control, they were calm, reflective and open. I left the country after that visit feeling deeply moved. I had witnessed the passing of a legend and had the opportunity to enjoy the energy in the air he left behind, redolent of peace and love.

Opinion leaders have written and spoken about Mandela's unparalleled leadership and sacrifice in the face of brutal opposition. They have expressed their admiration for his championship on the world stage of the plight of the oppressed. Two voices are representative of this tableau.

Richard Stengel, chief executive of the National Constitution Center from 2004–2006, *Time* magazine's managing editor from 2006–2013, and President Barack Obama's Under Secretary of State for Public Diplomacy and Public Affairs from 2014–2016, spent two years with Mandela working on Mandela's autobiography and got to know him quite well. In "Mandela: His 8 Lessons of Leadership," a *Time* magazine piece, Stengel (2008) refers to Mandela as a "secular saint" but a pragmatic problem solver as well. (I use this piece as a motivator for my students who are practicing to be school administrators, leading, as they will, school departments, buildings and districts.)

Stengel's article focuses on Mandela as a tactician, a brilliant strategist who knew how to move a political system through challenges. He observes:

> [Madiba's Rules] are mostly practical. Many of them stem from his personal experience. All of them are calibrated to cause the best kind of trouble: the trouble that forces us to ask how we can make the world a better place. (Stengel, 2008)

The lessons are powerful, and perhaps a bit surprising.
- Courage is not the absence of fear – it's inspiring others to move beyond it
- Lead from the front – but don't leave your base behind
- Lead from the back – and let others believe they are in front
- Know your enemy – and learn about his favorite sport
- Keep your friends close – and your rivals even closer
- Appearances matter – and remember to smile
- Nothing is black or white
- Quitting is leading too

Former United States President Barack Obama (2013) delivered a eulogy for Nelson Mandela which reflected Obama's deep, personal, abiding admiration for the South African leader. He was an inspiration for him. Obama's remarks were also political in that his message was, in part, for all to heed the alarm bell that Mandela rang ceaselessly: Pay attention to inequality wherever it may be housed and keep guard against the demise of equality wherever it might find a home.

Obama suggested that we are all allies in Mandela's struggles and triumphs. He was the curator of our deepest longings for a democratic way of life. After his long prison stay, he worked on fashioning a constitutional government which would work for all citizens now and in the future. He was committed to a rule of law which would provide for succession of power evidenced in his commitment to step down from the Presidency – and not, as many had predicted – become President for life.

Mandela was not afraid, Obama declared, to share his vulnerabilities with us. He insisted on sharing his triumphs along with his failures, his doubts and fears. "I'm not a saint," Mandela said, "unless you think of a sinner who keeps on trying." He earned his place in history through "struggle and shrewdness; persistence and faith."

In his remarks, Obama shared his belief there is no better statement of commitment than that found in Mandela's remarks made at his 1964 trial:

> I have fought against White domination and I have fought against Black domination. I've cherished the ideal of a democratic and free society in

which all persons live together in harmony and with equal opportunities. It is an ideal which I hope to live for and to achieve. But if needs be, it is an ideal for which I am prepared to die. (Mandela, 1964)

Obama opined: "He understood that ideas cannot be contained by prison walls, or extinguished by a sniper's bullet."

2 Dreaming

I have a dream that my four little children will one day live in a nation where they will not be judged by the color of their skin, but by the content of their character. (Martin Luther King, Jr.)

A Dream Deferred

What happens to a dream deferred?
Does it dry up
Like a raisin in the sun?
Or fester like a sore –
And then run?
Does it stink like rotten meat?
Or crust and sugar over –
like a syrupy sweet?
Maybe it just sags
like a heavy load.
Or does it explode?
(Langston Hughes)

Martin Luther King, Jr. was born on January 15, 1929, in Atlanta, Georgia, the second child of Martin Luther King Sr., a pastor, and Alberta Williams King, a former schoolteacher. He went to segregated public schools and attended Morehouse College where he studied medicine and law. MLK joined the ministry himself with the guidance of Morehouse's President, Dr. Benjamin Mays, a theologian and public advocate for racial equality. After graduating from Morehouse, King went on to earn a Bachelor of Divinity degree and eventually went on to earn a doctorate in systematic theology in 1955.

Martin Luther King, at an early age, became an icon of social justice advocacy. He led a bus boycott in Montgomery, Alabama, after Rosa Parks was arrested for refusing to give up her seat to a White passenger. A year later the

Supreme Court ruled that segregated bus seating was illegal. MLK's reputation had been established.

King's favorable repute also brought out the worst in the American public, being targeted, as he was, by White supremacists. His family home was firebombed soon after the court decision and, in September of 1958, while autographing books, he was stabbed in the chest. King survived and became an even more powerful proponent of non-violence for social change. This message was the foundation of his civil rights work for the rest of his life, including his stewardship of the SCLC (Southern Christian Leadership Conference). He credits Mahatma Gandhi's non-violent philosophy as the driving force behind SCLC and other initiatives he championed.

In 1963, King was arrested in Birmingham, Alabama, after participating in a non-violent protest – including a boycott, sit-ins, and marches – to protest segregation in a city rife with racial division. During his stay in prison, he penned what may be his most remarkable piece of writing, *Letter from a Birmingham Jail* (King, 1963). In it, he waxes eloquently and forcefully for the right to protest peacefully. This, as a response to public comments of concern and caution expressed by eight White religious leaders from the South.

> I must say to you that we have not made a single gain in civil rights without determined legal and nonviolent pressure. History is the long and tragic story of the fact that privileged groups seldom give up their privileges voluntarily. (King, 1963)

And then King, in a scathing rebuke of moderates, suggests that they may be more of a hindrance than a help to the cause. His comparisons and his conclusions are stunning.

> I MUST make two honest confessions to you, my Christian and Jewish brothers. First, I must confess that over the last few years I have been gravely disappointed with the White moderate. I have almost reached the regrettable conclusion that the Negro's great stumbling block in the stride toward freedom is not the White Citizens Councillor or the Ku Klux Klanner but the White moderate who is more devoted to order than to justice; who prefers a negative peace which is the absence of tension to a positive peace which is the presence of justice; who constantly says, "I agree with you in the goal you seek, but I can't agree with your methods of direct action"; who paternalistically feels that he can set the timetable for another man's freedom; who lives by the myth of time; and who constantly advises the Negro to wait until a "more convenient season."

> Shallow understanding from people of good will is more frustrating than absolute misunderstanding from people of ill will. Lukewarm acceptance is much more bewildering than outright rejection. (King, 1963)

Continuing his brash campaign that garnered worldwide attention, he helped to organize the *March on Washington for Jobs and Freedom* in 1963. The event shone a brilliant light on the struggles of African Americans for equal opportunity and justice in the United States. Attended by 200,000–300,000 people, the event marked an inflection point in the movement, stimulating the passage of the Civil Rights Act of 1964. It also gave King his largest platform yet to espouse his message. His most famous speech, "I Have a Dream," occupies a prominent position in the annals of great American oration. Another milestone event, capturing worldwide attention and inspired by King and other civil rights leaders, the Selma to Montgomery march (aka Bloody Sunday), was the scene of peaceful protestors being attacked by state troopers and county posse men with billy clubs and tear gas. The protestors were demanding fairness in voting for people of color. Southern state legislatures, despite the 1964 Civil Rights Act, were passing discriminatory regulations that denied most African Americans the right to vote. After a series of follow-up marches, the Voting Rights Act was passed on August 6, 1965.

Martin Luther King was assassinated in April of 1968 by James Earl Ray, a known racist and escaped convict, as he stood on the balcony of a motel in Memphis, Tennessee. King had traveled there to provide support for a sanitation workers' strike.

King's son, Martin Luther King III, was interviewed 56 years after his father's "Dream" speech. He was frank in his remarks, offering that elements of his father's dream have come true, yet saying he had hoped we would be much further along as a nation. He suggests that the US is undergoing a "metamorphosis," believing that all of the negative has to come out if the positive is to emerge. We, our nation, thought that racism was resolved, we thought civil rights issues were resolved – certainly we did 10–12 years ago – especially after the election of President Obama. He didn't think we lived in a post-racial society at the time, but he thought we had come further. It feels now like we have gone back to the 1950s. However, Martin Luther King III is optimistic that with others calling for a revolution of values, as his father did, and finding a universal tone that everyone can relate to, as his father did, we can be successful in our quest for social justice. We need to work collectively. It is not the single individual, but the coalition of organizations that will lead the way (Hassan, 2019).

In his last book, *Chaos or Community?* (1967), Dr. King warned that the movement was already hobbled by delusion. "The majority of White

Americans consider themselves sincerely committed to justice for the Negro," he wrote.

> They believe that American society is essentially hospitable to fair play and to steady growth toward a middle-class utopia embodying racial harmony. But, unfortunately, this is a fantasy of self-deception and comfortable vanity. (Muhammad, 2017)

Martin Luther King weighed in on South African issues in a speech he delivered in 1964 in London on his way to receive the Nobel Peace Prize in Oslo.[1] His remarks reflect a passion – and empathy – for the oppressed in South Africa and some suggestions for support from other countries. He talked about the long and painful struggle for freedom and justice in the US, and how US citizens feel a sense of identity with the South African struggle for freedom, which he characterized as "far more deadly." He cited Mississippi experiences fighting for justice as a reminder of South African issues, although he made a clear distinction between the two contexts:

> ... yet even in Mississippi we can organize to register Negro voters, we can speak to the press, we can, in short, organize the people in non-violent action. But, in South Africa even the mildest form of non-violent resistance meets with years of imprisonment, and leaders over many years have been restricted and silenced and imprisoned. (King, n.d.)

He suggested that given the untenable situation in South Africa where people are "... denied their humanity, their dignity, denied opportunity, denied all human rights ... with many of the bravest and best South Africans serving long years in prison, with some already executed ..." (King, n.d.), both his country and the United Kingdom might be able to change the situation through economic pressure by boycotting South African goods. His belief was that the pressure would end apartheid. "Then the majority of South Africans of all races could at last build the shared society they desire" (King, n.d.). Divestment campaigns against South Africa, which originated in the 1960s, and were organized throughout the Western world – the United States officially participating in the mid-1980s – were largely thought to be the precipitating force which contributed to the demise of the apartheid system.

A unique perspective on MLK, perhaps, is offered in the book, *The Radical King*, edited by Cornel West (King, 2016). West, in an introduction to the book, acquaints us with the Martin Luther King who was akin to, but different from, many of his popular representations. West says:

King indeed had a dream. King's dream was rooted in the American Dream – it was what the quest for life, liberty, and the pursuit of happiness looked like for people enslaved and Jim Crowed, terrorized, traumatized, and stigmatized by American laws and American citizens. (King, 2016 p. xi)

He continues, offering bold characterizations of King, inviting us to become acquainted with the "radical" King. He asserts: "King's dream of a more free and democratic America and world had morphed into, in his words, 'a nightmare,' owing to the persistence of 'racism, poverty, militarism, and materialism.' He called America a 'sick society'" (King, 2016, p. xi). The radical King was a "warrior for peace" on both domestic and global battlefronts, a staunch critic of colonial and imperial power. His commitment to non-violence was designed to challenge the spread of worldwide militarism. He was a "spiritual giant" who confronted the callousness and indifference of his countrymen. He believed that "indifference to evil is more evil than evil itself." The radical King was a "moral titan" who was genuinely committed to the dignity of people of all colors. His struggle against White supremacy was "never a strategic move or tactical afterthought; rather it was a profound existential and moral matter of great urgency." The radical King was a "democratic socialist" who fought for the poor in a class struggle for "resources, power and space" (King, 2016, pp. xi–xiii).

3   The Torch Passed

The oracular spirit remains alive. Once touched by the magic of MLK and Mandela's conviction, others carry on the work. Some with sensational clarity and volume, able to articulate the message on the public stage, and others with quiet courage, fortified by the power of righteousness. In my travels in both countries, I meet many who are committed to shifting the social spheres towards more equity. They include leaders of advocacy groups, educational administrators, teachers, students, community organizers, among others. These people maintain the social engines that continue the fight towards justice for all. The fuel is combustible: integrity, passion, sacrifice, courage. One can almost hear Mandela and MLK cheering in the background.

I was a visitor in a University of Stellenbosch class, an experience I referenced in an earlier chapter. The lesson focused on the history of colonial invasions and disruptions of native South African peoples. The professor challenged the students – an almost exclusively White group which filled a lecture hall – to confront the reality of the racist and violent incursions into their country by those who considered native Africans to be less than human and to ask: "What can I do now to make right what was so wrong?" He referenced "martyrological" memories (Jansen, 2009), i.e., something from the past memory, within an ecclesiastical or secular context, that you're willing to die for. (A hagiography of Nelson Mandela is rife with examples.) The bar is set high, he suggested, the work is daunting, but the calling is in each of us if we listen for it. I felt I was witnessing a sermon – in this case a secular one – that challenged the assembled to fight the good fight as they go out into the wider world. The torch was offered that day to hundreds of young people.

4   A Traveler's Guide through the Arc of the Moral Universe

Dr. King often ended his comments about fighting for the cause of social justice with this phrase: "The moral arc of the universe bends at the elbow of justice."

King's sentiment, which is also found in the speeches of Abraham Lincoln, was inspired by comments first voiced by Theodore Parker. Parker was a minister in the Unitarian church in the mid-1800s who espoused an optimistic outlook towards the eventual success of abolitionist causes. A more complete text of his remarks illuminates the message grandly.

> I do not pretend to understand the moral universe; the arc is a long one, my eye reaches but little ways; I cannot calculate the curve and complete the figure by the experience of sight; I can divine it by conscience. And from what I see I am sure it bends towards justice.

Parker's message, popularized as it was by Dr. King, serves as a reminder that when the going gets rough, when the odds are against those who fight for equality, the work will eventually be rewarded – justice will prevail. This optimism has become a clarion call for me as I pursue my work.

In a graduate course I teach – for those aspiring to be school leaders – I ask students to complete an exercise in which they chart a course from problem to resolution. The problem can be anything that might arise in the daily administration of a school: a discipline issue, a teacher contract dispute, suspicion of parent abuse/neglect of a child, issues involving sexism and racism, etc. I ask them to move along a continuum, imagining stops along the way to refresh their resolve and gather information to be better informed. Each stop is framed by a theme, e.g., collaboration, research, communications, etc. Eventually, they produce a running record of their travels, detailing how they changed course at times, needed a full stop every now and then, and, generally, navigated the terrain. I ask them to use values-driven principles of educational leadership and note the principles used at various points. I call the lesson *A School Leader's GPS* (Guide for Public Schools).

What would this exercise look like if the trip involved traversing the moral arc of the universe, with guidance provided by the wisdom of Mandela and King? In this case, the demarcation points might be identified by the moral imperatives of the journey. To chart the course, see the stopping points/turning points below, with advice from your travel agents, Nelson and Martin.

Justice

Injustice anywhere is a threat to justice everywhere. (MLK)

Now is the time to lift our national policy from the quicksand of racial injustice to the solid rock of human dignity. (MLK)

As long as poverty, injustice and gross inequality persist in our world, none of us can truly rest. (Mandela)

Courage

The ultimate measure of a man is not where he stands in moments of comfort and convenience, but where he stands at times of challenge and controversy. (MLK)

Freedom is never voluntarily given by the oppressor; it must be demanded by the oppressed. (MLK)

Our lives begin to end the day we become silent about things that matter. (MLK)

I learned that courage was not the absence of fear, but the triumph over it. The brave man is not he who does not feel afraid, but he who conquers that fear. (Mandela)

Part of being optimistic is keeping one's head pointed toward the sun, one's feet moving forward. There were many dark moments when my faith in humanity was sorely tested, but I would not and could not give myself up to despair. That way lays to defeat and death. (Mandela)

Education

Without education, your children can never really meet the challenges they will face. So it's very important to give children education and explain that they should play a role for their country. (Mandela)

The function of education is to teach one to think intensively and to think critically. Intelligence plus character - that is the goal of true education. (MLK)

Truth

I believe that unarmed truth and unconditional love will have the final word in reality. This is why right, temporarily defeated, is stronger than evil triumphant. (MLK)

I can't pretend that I'm brave and that I can beat the whole world. (Mandela)

Love

Darkness cannot drive out darkness; only light can do that. Hate cannot drive out hate; only love can do that. (MLK)

I have decided to stick with love. Hate is too great a burden to bear. (MLK)

If you talk to a man in a language he understands, that goes to his head. If you talk to him in his language,that goes to his heart. (Mandela)

Our human compassion binds us the one to the other - not in pity or patronizingly, but as human beings who have learnt how to turn our common suffering into hope for the future. (Mandela)

Service

They have carved a tunnel of hope through the dark mountain of disappointment. (Referring to those who fought and sacrificed in the civil rights movement.) (MLK)

Everybody can be great ... because anybody can serve. You don't have to have a college degree to serve. You don't have to make your subject and verb agree to serve. You only need a heart full of grace. A soul generated by love. (MLK)

There is nothing I fear more than waking up without a program that will help me bring a little happiness to those with no resources, those who are poor, illiterate, and ridden with terminal disease. (Mandela)

Life's most persistent and urgent question is, 'What are you doing for others?' (MLK)

Forgiveness

As I walked out the door toward the gate that would lead to my freedom, I knew if I didn't leave my bitterness and hatred behind, I'd still be in prison. (Mandela)

If there are dreams about a beautiful South Africa, there are also roads that lead to their goal. Two of these roads could be named Goodness and Forgiveness. (Mandela)

We must develop and maintain the capacity to forgive. He who is devoid of the power to forgive is devoid of the power to love. There is some good in the worst of us and some evil in the best of us. When we discover this, we are less prone to hate our enemies. (MLK)

5   Mandela and King as Change Agents: Caveat Emptor

The iconic leadership of Nelson Mandela and Martin Luther King Jr. provides an unmatched civic fable for their respective countries. However, the citizens of South Africa and the US would be advised to note that there is risk involved in too much faith being placed in their singular achievements. There is no guarantee that comes along with the attendant promise of extraordinary leaders, even those who have been martyred. Those who reap the benefits of change have a responsibility to *maintain* the goods. The improvements are not sustainable without attention.

MLK and Mandela were heroes in the fight for equality in their countries – and around the world. By any measure, they impacted the lives of millions through their public virtue. But, their clarion call for justice is hardly the end of the line. "Mission accomplished"? Perhaps "mission begun" would be more accurate.

Despite enormous strides towards equality, both countries still have dark clouds of oppression hanging over them. The new iteration is slick. The rich and powerful have changed the laws, have installed policies and practices that prohibit overt discrimination, i.e., taken the "Colored only"/"White only" signs off the bathroom doors. Nevertheless, they have managed to provide a clear road map for some, so that they – and they alone – can locate and enjoy the best resources. Others are left to fend for themselves. All the while the new leaders claim that they see no color. They are good to go with equality. All are welcome. No pass cards needed.

A pledge might be in order for those who are skeptics: Let's issue a warning label on the "job completed" banner that so many wave when asked about the progress made to eliminate the racial divide. We owe it to Nelson and Martin to recognize that, although their work was masterful – and changed much – we are in a sanitized mode which demands our attention.

Note

1   King's speech was retrieved from the *Democracy Now* website (https://www.democracynow.org/2015/1/19/exclusive_newly_discovered_1964_mlk_speech) which stores a video copy of the speech.

CHAPTER 9

Hope

Nelson Mandela and Martin Luther King were the standard bearers of movements to topple White supremacy doctrines in their countries. They used an unparalleled passion and an incomparable eloquence to implore their fellow citizens to rise up against tyranny and demand equality for all. The struggle, of course, continues.

After the cruelty, after the divisions, after the hatred, after the despair, where are we now? Are we in the midst of a cease-fire? Does the battle still rage, the artillery now hidden in the covert social spaces that control the destinies of different groups of people? Those who seem bent on preserving the privilege that some have and denying the truth about the continuing divides will be satisfied with the status quo. On the other hand, those who know there is a better way, have been, and will be, mustering support for a brighter future for all. Those who live and breathe and radiate the message of equality will not be diverted from the cause. They will continue to serve as role models for the rest of us.

There are reasons to be hopeful.

1   The Pride of Lions

> The truth is like a lion. You don't have to defend it. Let it loose. It will defend itself. (St. Augustine)

> A small body of determined spirits fired by an unquenchable faith in their mission can alter the course of history. (Gandhi)

Maya Angelou delivers an unsanitized message about oppression in her poetry. She stirs the soul with her powerful language and her unrelenting drum beat. Here she pens a note to her oppressors. They may try to silence her or make her second class. They won't succeed.

Still I Rise

You may write me down in history
With your bitter, twisted lies,

© KONINKLIJKE BRILL NV, LEIDEN, 2020 | DOI: 10.1163/9789004444430_009

You may trod me in the very dirt
But still, like dust, I'll rise.

Does my sassiness upset you?
Why are you beset with gloom?
'Cause I walk like I've got oil wells
Pumping in my living room.

Just like moons and like suns,
With the certainty of tides,
Just like hopes springing high,
Still I'll rise.

Did you want to see me broken?
Bowed head and lowered eyes?
Shoulders falling down like teardrops,
Weakened by my soulful cries?

Does my haughtiness offend you?
Don't you take it awful hard
'Cause I laugh like I've got gold mines
Diggin' in my own backyard.

You may shoot me with your words,
You may cut me with your eyes,
You may kill me with your hatefulness,
But still, like air, I'll rise.

Does my sexiness upset you?
Does it come as a surprise
That I dance like I've got diamonds
At the meeting of my thighs?

Out of the huts of history's shame
I rise
Up from a past that's rooted in pain
I rise
I'm a black ocean, leaping and wide,
Welling and swelling I bear in the tide.

Leaving behind nights of terror and fear
I rise
Into a daybreak that's wondrously clear
I rise
Bringing the gifts that my ancestors gave,
I am the dream and the hope of the slave.
I rise
I rise
I rise.
(Maya Angelou)

Maya Angelou's assertions through poetry are breathtaking – and a call to action. An equally potent challenge originates – in another context – from the work of Paulo Freire who confronts the social dynamics of oppression. In a tribute to the power of strategic planning, Freire suggests that smart leadership can offer the calculus necessary for the oppressed to become free. In *Pedagogy of Hope* (1992), he recounts his interactions with a Portuguese guest workers' neighborhood in a German community. The workers were being exploited by the landlords (of their shacks) who avoided tenant laws and the rights and obligations they had towards their tenants and who charged them exorbitant rental fees. Organizers went into action, with other representatives of the community, to protest the landlords' actions – complaints in the newspapers, fliers, and walks through the community. The local priest, a member of the group that coordinated the protest movement, shared that he was approached by one of the victims and asked to call off the action. The man was threatened with eviction by his landlord, unless he stopped the accusations. The priest decided to call off the protest in deference to those being intimidated by the unabashed cruelty of the landlords.

Freire concludes that here was another example of the oppressed being intimidated and the leaders of a protest frustrated. He concludes that the priest did the right thing. By calling a halt to the action, the priest had time to work with his community on overcoming the fear. When victims see the oppressor as "unbeatable" they have less of a tendency to believe in themselves. By educating the public about the vulnerabilities of the oppressor, i.e., understanding the "mechanisms of social conflict," "the weakness of the oppressed turns into strength capable of converting the oppressors' strength into weakness. This is a hope that moves us" (Freire, 1992, p. 108).

Angelou calls out for anger and resolve in the face of oppression. Freire asks us to consider strategic responses to clear and present dangers. There are others who call for disrupting the status quo as essential for change. William Booth, founder of the Salvation Army, proclaims "You cannot improve the future without disturbing the present." The poet and playwright Oscar Wilde, in the late 1800's, said "Disobedience, in the eyes of anyone who has read history, is man's original virtue. It is through disobedience that progress has been made, through disobedience and through rebellion."

Neville Alexander (a political activist, author, and teacher – and a prisoner on Robben Island with Mandela), when he was Director of the Project for the Study of Alternative Education in South Africa, weighed in on the responsibility of leadership to change the social order:

> ... social identities are historical, not primordial ... To take the attitude that the question of social identities is best left alone or, worse, that the inherited identities should be allowed to perpetuate themselves, is to abdicate the responsibility of leadership and to commit oneself to maintaining the older order in all but name. (Alexander, 2004)

In a speech to the United Nations General Assembly in 2014, anti-apartheid activist Ahmed Kathrada, asks us to build a worldwide coalition, a "global campaign," to confront racism. "In this way, maybe the dream of a 'Greenpeace' against racism could become a reality" (Kathrada, n.d.).

And then there are those who have drawn a bright line between themselves and moral compromise. We hear in their voices a deeply felt commitment to change. We are assured that there are those who will brook no compromise. If we look carefully, we will find others who are equally devoted to doing the right thing, despite the consequences. There is hope here.

> I will stay in jail to the end of my days before I make a butchery of my conscience. (John Bunyan, English writer and Puritan preacher, mid-1600s)

> Let them call me rebel and welcome, I feel no concern from it; but I should suffer the misery of devils, were I to make a whore of my soul .... (Thomas Paine, political activist, philosopher and revolutionary, mid-1700s)

Metaphors seem to come naturally to express the resolve to change things. Herewith, my contributions:

> The arsenal of social weaponry we draw upon to combat the forces of injustice is stocked with tools forged from a variety of raw materials.

This factory, built on the genius of invention for change, augers well for a brighter future. As a testament to our hard work and as a keepsake for future generations, we paint murals on the factory walls with hopeful pictures that reflect fundamental change, a chiaroscuro portrait with distributions of all colors of the rainbow.

As a final thought on this subject: My wife and I visited a petting zoo in Johannesburg where we were able to hold lion cubs in our arms and feed them bottles of milk. They were cuddly, warm, and defenseless.

When the lions are unleashed, beware those who prey on their babies.

2   Messages from the Field

In my travels to various locales in both South Africa and the US, I was on the lookout for examples of strength and courage, resolve and aspiration to make a brighter future for all. I found many hopeful signs.

A former principal, now professional developer, said:

> The human spirit will prevail! Human history is replete with fights against gross violations of human rights. We continue the fight today. We do have to be careful of normalization because it can lead to inaction and blindness of our current reality. We need to be acutely aware of continuing inequalities despite progress.

And in an example of jumping to conclusions – based on prejudices – I was eating breakfast in a lovely hotel in Stellenbosch. A loud, obnoxious White man was sitting with his wife eating breakfast not far from me. I thought for sure he was a racist since I heard snippets of conversation about their journeys around the world. Snippets that I *imagined* had racial implications. His tones seemed angry. (I assumed that an agitated, loud White man in South Africa would have to be racist.) I happened to start a conversation with him. Turns out he and his wife are part of a group that feeds homeless people around the world. They were devoted to, in fact had dedicated their lives to, eradicating hunger, not with filling their stomachs with eggs, bacon, muffins – and hate – as I had presumed.

I found remarks by a New York State administrator who oversees special programs, were important to reflect upon. "As long as we have the 'open wound' of racism we will not heal. We may have a scab on top, but it is also infected and keeps oozing up." He added a warning: "In the absence of hope, anarchy is right around the corner." All the more reason to encourage, promote, and defend those who organize for change.

A sampling of my notes during a visit to a primary school in Soweto, the largest South African township, tells a story of the strength of the human spirit in the face of unspeakably difficult challenges. In a class of 60 fourth graders, the teacher was doing a mathematics lesson and she asked me if I would teach a portion of the lesson. The kids could not have been more cooperative – and patient – with my impromptu lesson plan. Afterwards, the students had an informal conversation with me. They asked me questions about America and I asked them about South Africa. They thanked me for coming and wished me a "nice flight" home. Then a student raised her hand to ask this extraordinary question: "When did you realize you had the potential to be a teacher?" (Those were her exact words!)

We walked into another class – it was either fourth or fifth grade – and the teacher asked if I wouldn't mind asking the students some questions. Be happy to, I answered. How many of you will be going to university? (All hands went up.) What do you want to be when you grow up? Answers included: a pilot, a lawyer, a doctor, a biomechanical engineer, a rheumatologist, a teacher, a famous writer, and on and on in this vein.

In a university class in Stellenbosch, the professor ended his lecture about oppression with this promise: "I want to make you all social justice warriors." The mostly White audience applauded.

In the US, I observed an event in the auditorium of a high school with a student population that is virtually all Black and Hispanic. The assembly program featured a student panel discussion about contemporary issues. At one point, they were asked what they would like to do in the wider world. Almost all responses were higher-level professional jobs. One boy said he wanted to be President of the United States. He conveyed a power from the stage – a star athlete with a gleaming presence. And, he was extraordinarily articulate and insightful when he spoke during the discussion. I had a chance to speak with him afterwards. I told him that I wished I could change the law so that a person could be elected President before the age of 35. That's how impressed I was. Turns out the administrators and teachers felt the same way about him.

(So happens I asked a group of secondary students in Johannesburg the same question: What would they like to do in the wider world? Their answers were equally mighty regarding their career aspirations. And, one student said he would like to be President of South Africa.)

How's that for hope for the future?

3   Why Try?

How does one answer the question "Why try?" to those reluctant to participate
in a makeover of the social schema? A few examples – regarding the US school
system – may be the start of a conversation.

It has been shown that improved academic outcomes for all students can
be found in integrated school systems. These students are more likely to find
good jobs, have higher educational attainment overall, have better incomes,
and more opportunities to choose good neighborhoods to raise their families.
"They are more likely to choose to live in an integrated neighborhood, in part,
because their interracial contact experiences in integrated K-12 schools and
colleges broke the intergenerational transmission of racial prejudice and fear"
(Mickelson, 2011). They are also willing to enroll their children in integrated
schools, knowing how they benefited from the experience.

In these ways "… integrated schools and neighborhoods are likely to foster
a mutually reinforcing intergenerational cycle across the life-course that
advances social cohesion in a multiethnic democratic society and promotes
racial equality" (Mickelson, 2011).

Student achievement is higher in integrated schools for kids of color as well.
While evidence points to the academic benefits of an integrated school program, there is also research to support the long-term social benefits of an integrated experience. Racially integrated schools are less likely to engage in racial
stereotyping; there is more cross-racial understanding amongst students.
Children who attend these schools at a younger age are particularly prone to
this disposition. In sharp contrast, those who have spent most of their public
school and college experiences in segregated settings are more likely to have
internalized racial stereotypes. These young people are more likely to live in
segregated neighborhoods as well and have little chance to break down the
walls they've erected.

School desegregation has little or no effect on White student test scores as
measured against all-White school student achievement. In addition, students
in the integrated settings are able to more easily recognize the existence and
effects of discrimination on other students. They are more tolerant – and inclusive – of groups their friends belong to. The exposure of students to others who
are not of their racial background creates an element of comfort and safety
when they do engage individuals of other backgrounds. When students have
positive social and psychological experiences in school they tend to perform
better academically as well.[1]

Lastly, the society-at-large benefits from integrated school settings. The progress of the nation can improve when there exists an embracing of differences. We need leaders who understand and embrace difference, especially in the raw and ugly moments of calculated bigotry that we have recently witnessed. The reach of the benefits goes beyond our shores. A more engaged citizenry and productive workforce – coming as a result of an increased understanding of diverse communities – is an important asset for all of our citizens in an increasing multicultural and global environment.[2]

A related personal experience fits well here. I visited a school in the United States that has one of the best reputations in the country. It offers premiere facilities, e.g., athletic fields that rival professional settings, and achievement scores that are at the top of the heap. And, the student body is virtually all White. I spoke with the principal, who, of course, was very proud of his students' accomplishments. However, it was not lost on him that the student body did not reflect the demographics of the wider world. In fact, he thought it his obligation to share with parents that they should seriously consider exposing their children to more multi-cultural experiences so that they would be better prepared to interact with people of all colors and backgrounds. He did not have to make the suggestion; it could have backfired in some cases. He didn't care. It was his obligation to deliver the message anyway.

4   Organizing for Change

A myriad of organizations worldwide are focused on reducing, if not eliminating, racial tensions and divisions. A sampling of these stout efforts is heartening.

The Center for Third World Organizing (CTWO) is a racial-justice organization dedicated to building a social-justice movement led by people of color. As a training and resource center, it promotes and sustains direct-action organizing in communities of color in the United States. CTWO's programs include training of new and experienced organizers; establishing model multi-racial community organizations; and building an active network of organizations and activists of color to achieve racial justice in its fullest dimensions. (This description from the *Racial Equity Resource Guide*[3] found on-line.)

The Anti-Racism Network South Africa (ARNSA) was established by the Ahmed Kathrada and Nelson Mandela Foundations in 2015. Its secretariat also includes the Institute for Justice and Reconciliation (IJR), and the Centre for the Advancement of Non-Racialism and Democracy (CANRAD). A number of other organizations in various provinces are part of the network. The network aims to ensure that local organizations are capacitated to deal with issues of racism within communities, but at the same time, form part of national and international efforts to tackle the scourge. (This description from the *ARNSA*[4] website.)

I have had the distinct pleasure – and honor – to become personally acquainted with two local organizations doing extraordinary work on Long Island and in Johannesburg, *ERASE RACISM* and *TOMORROW TRUST*, respectively.

ERASE RACISM[5] focuses on racial divide issues needing attention in the Long Island area, just outside New York City. Their initiatives include: The Inclusive Housing Program, which addresses housing discrimination. (Policy advocacy, community organizing, and legal action are their tools.) The Education Equity Initiative, which focuses on unequal access to quality public schools by working to increase opportunities for Black and Latino students to attend high quality schools, as well as promoting racially diverse schools for all students. I have attended numerous workshops and participated in action-oriented public presentations with *ERASE RACISM*. They are a spirited group of focused individuals, headed by a long-standing leader of strong conviction and energy, who enjoys a large and vocal following and are often consulted first when the media are covering a story on racial issues.

The Tomorrow Trust[6] is a non-profit organization based in South Africa which supports orphaned and other vulnerable children throughout their education, providing academics, life skills, and self-development, so that they can reach their full potential and become self-sustaining and proactive members of society. They provide support for students from the earliest stages of education through adulthood. Alumni are encouraged to give back to fellow students in younger grades and contribute to the well-being of children in similar circumstances. I have visited *The Tomorrow Trust* classes on several occasions. The teachers are remarkably committed to the project. The students take their work seriously and offer insights that are well beyond their years. The organization is headed up by extraordinary individuals who have the grit and stamina to work in an extremely challenging environment.

5   The Spirit of Ubuntu – I Am, Because We Are

Over the last 12 years, I have listened to and observed the work of many who are deeply committed to the cause of eliminating racial divides that plague our world. They have laudable plans and strategies that are necessary to meeting their goals. They are focused individuals with passion. As I end my reflections on their work and the background and contexts they work in, I would like to share a larger frame of reference – Ubuntu. I believe this concept propels the work and should accompany the service. A brief excerpt from the Obama eulogy for Mandela in 2013, succinctly defines its meaning.

> Mandela understood the ties that bind the human spirit. There is a word in South Africa – Ubuntu – that describes his greatest gift: his recognition that we are all bound together in ways that can be invisible to the eye; that there is a oneness to humanity; that we achieve ourselves by sharing ourselves with others, and caring for those around us. (Obama, 2013)

And, for further clarification, here are examples from everyday practitioners of Ubuntu.

As I was preparing to leave a 4th grade class in SOWETO, the teacher asked the students if they wanted to say anything to me. Here's a sample of what I heard: "Have a safe trip home"; "We appreciated you coming to see us"; "I love you and God Bless You"; "I love you like a father." They also sang songs to me. One was awe-inspiring. It was a song about how we need to love one another and then we can love the whole world!

I spent time in a classroom in an elementary school on Long Island. We were discussing the South Africa project. Students were enthusiastic about making connections with a school – their partner school – in South Africa. They drew and wrote messages to their "friends" in the Marvin Park Primary School. One little boy, as he drew a picture for a boy in South Africa, said to me: "I used to have two brothers, now I have three."

Sara Lawrence-Lightfoot, the distinguished scholar who has examined social and cultural relationships as they affect schools, suggests a tool that might assist us in getting the Ubuntu spirit rolling. "Empathic Attunement" offers the following advice for beginning to understand 'the other':

> Take a 'bite' out of someone else and appreciate him/her; acknowledge the pain; maintain a position of not knowing; act with reverence and awe." She adds ingredients along the way: "Be visible; make everyone visible; risk discomfort and vulnerability to get to the truth; break away from "clannishness"; places that exclude are impoverished; winning and losing is a harsh paradigm. (Lawrence-Lightfoot, 2016)

Sociologist Neville Alexander, the widely known South African intellectual and activist referenced earlier, trumpets this pronouncement about the world as community, the spirit of Ubuntu in action:

> ... it is high time that we plan for a second Copernican revolution. This is a revolution in the conceptual universe that will populate the heads of

the coming generations, no longer cluttered with superstitions such as 'race', caste and reified 'ethnicity.' (Alexander, 2004)

6   A Last Word

I have attempted in this book to explicate the troubles I have seen, read about, and researched in both South Africa and my home country regarding continuing racial divides. I have posed more questions than answers, I am sure. In a deeply moving – prophetic? – coincidence, as I was completing this last chapter, not looking for any particular reference, I came across this poem.

Question and Answer

Durban, Birmingham,
Cape Town, Atlanta,
Johannesburg, Watts,
The earth around
Struggling, fighting,
Dying – for what?

A world to gain.

Groping, hoping,
Waiting – for what?

A world to gain.

Dreams kicked asunder,
Why not go under?

There's a world to gain.

But suppose I don't want it,
Why take it?

To remake it.
(Langston Hughes)

That about says it all.

Notes

1 Many of the benefits of integration/desegregation mentioned in this section can be found in a 2017 publication by ERASE Racism, *A Decade of Change: Growing School Segregation on Long Island.*

2 A determined initiative that bears review is *The Civil Rights Project*, housed in UCLA, which examines critical issues of civil rights and equal opportunity for racial and ethnic groups in the US (https://civilrightsproject.ucla.edu/).

3 The guide referred to can be found at http://www.racialequityresourceguide.org/ The purpose of the guide is unique, as explained on the site: *The directory of materials found on this site have been prepared as a shared tool for building a community of connected, informed and engaged practitioners. With the ability to generate a Resource Guide tailored to their own goals, these materials are practical resources that will assist organizations working within the racial healing and racial equity field.*

4 The ARNSA website (https://www.arnsa.org.za/home) provides a trove of anti-racism resources. The mission is stated on the site: "The network aims to ensure that local organisations are capacitated to deal with issues of racism within communities, but at the same time, form part of national and international efforts to tackle the scourge."

5 From the EraseRacism (http://www.eraseracismny.org/) website: "ERASE Racism is a regional organization that leads public policy advocacy campaigns and related initiatives to promote racial equity in areas such as housing, public school education, and community development. We engage in a variety of research, education and consulting activities to address institutional and structural racism."

6 The Tomorrow Trust website (https://www.tomorrow.org.za/) explains the organization's lofty pursuit: "We are dedicated to finding the students who are the most vulnerable and marginalized, and who therefore have the greatest potential to change the course of their futures. We evaluate each student as whole individuals – individuals who have intricate and specialized needs that cannot be met by a "one size fits all" mentality towards education.

References

Agosto, V. (2014). Scripted curriculum: What movies teach about dis/ability and Black males. *Teachers College Record, 116*. doi:https://eric.ed.gov/?id=EJ1020239

Albrecht, L. (2012, February 24). Book review of fire in the heart: How White activists embrace racial justice. *Teachers College Record*. Retrieved from https://www.tcrecord.org/
content.asp?contentid=16714

Alexander, N. (2004). *Implications of brown v board of education: A post-apartheid South African perspective*. Project for the Study of Alternative Education in South Africa (PRAESA).

Alexander, M. (2010). *The new Jim Crow: Mass incarceration in the age of colorblindness*. The New Press.

Anderson, C. (2017). *White rage: The unspoken truth of our racial divide*. Bloomsbury.

Arendt, H. (1963). *Eichmann in Jerusalem: A report on the banality of evil*. Viking Press.

Banaji, M. R., & Greenwald, A. G. (2016). *Blind spot: Hidden biases of good people*. Bantam Books.

Bass, L. (2014). Interview with Sonya Dounglass Horsford. The more things change, the more they stay the same: Reflecting on brown v. board of education, 60 years later. *University Council for Educational Administration, 55*(3), 20–23.

Bass, L. (2014). Interview with Sonya Douglass Horsford. *University Council for Educational Administration, 55*(3), 20–23.

Beaubien, J. (2018, April 2). *The country with the world's worst inequality is ...* Retrieved from https://www.npr.org/sections/goatsandsoda/2018/04/02/598864666/the-country-with-the-worlds-worst-inequality-isnprspecialreport

Bell, D. (1992). *Faces at the bottom of the well*. Basic Books.

Berliner, D. (2013). Effects of inequality and poverty vs. teachers and schooling on America's youth. *Teachers College Record, 115*(12). Retrieved from https://www.tcrecord.org/content.asp?contentid=16889

Berry, E. M., & Yang, C. (2019, July 7). The dominance of the White male critic. *The New York Times*, p. 10.

Boddy-Evans, A. (2019, March 29). *Quotes from PW Botha, Prime Minister of South Africa*. Retrieved from https://www.thoughtco.com/quotes-pw-botha-43577

Boomer, G. (1992). *Negotiating the curriculum: Educating for the 21st century* (G. Boomer, N. Lester, C. Onore, & J. Cook, Eds.). Falmer.

Breda, D. T. (2019, February 21). Fight linguistic terrorism. *Cape Argus*, p. 9.

Bronner, E. (2014, July 13). A damaging distance. *The New York Times*, p. 3.

Brown, E. (2016, April 20). A Black professor offers advice 'for White folks who teach in the hood'. *The Washington Post*.

Brown, V. (2017, February 28). *South African men and women involved in the skin bleaching scandal*. Retrieved from https://www.news.com.au/lifestyle/beauty/face-body/ south-african-men-and-women-involved-in-the-skin-bleaching-scandal/news-story/e2928e91b2754ce53c80b6ccb762eb0d

Buber, M. (1970). *I and thou*. Charles Scribners Sons.

Cape Argus. (2019, July 29). *How apartheid still haunts education system*. Amnesty International. Retrieved from https://www.iol.co.za/news/south-africa/gauteng/ how-apartheid-still-haunts-education-system-amnesty-international-30021880

Carter, P. L. (2012). *Stubborn roots: Race, culture, and inequality in U.S. and South African schools*. Oxford University Press.

Child, K. (2013, December 6). SA education gets an F mark. *The Times*, pp. 1–2.

Child, K. (2018, January 7). *Cutting through the matric results spin – The real facts*. Retrieved from https://www.businesslive.co.za/bd/national/2018-01-07-cutting-through-the-matric-results-spin--the-real-facts/

Chutel, L. (2017, August 25). *Post-apartheid South Africa is failing the very people it liberated*. Retrieved from https://qz.com/africa/1061461/post-apartheid-south-africa-is-failing-the-very-people-it-liberated/

Cohen, P. (2010, October 18). 'Culture of poverty,' long an academic Slur, makes a comeback. *The New York Times*, pp. A1–A16.

Collins, C. S., & Jun, A. (2017). *White out: Understanding White privilege and dominance in the modern age*. Peter Lang.

Constas, M. (1996). Apartheid and the socio-political context of education in South Africa: A narrative account. *Teachers College Record, 98*(4), 682–720.

Cooper, H. (2016, November 27). What is the color of beauty? Popular skin-lightening products and mixed messages in West Africa. *The New York Times*, pp. 1, 12–13.

Darder, A. (2015, April). *Cultural hegemony, language & politics of forgetting: Interrogating restrictive language policies*. Paper presented at AERA Annual Conference.

Dawsey, J. (2018, January 12). Trump derides protections for immigrants from "shithole" countries. *The Washington Post*. Retrieved from https://www.washingtonpost.com/ politics/trump-attacks-protections-for-immigrants-from-shithole-countries-in-oval-office-meeting/2018/01/11/bfc0725c-f711-11e7-91af-31ac729add94_story.html

Dearstyne, B. W. (2019, February 16). *Whose country is this?* Trump, Coolidge and Immigration. Retrieved from https://historynewsnetwork.org/article/171187

DeGruy, J. (2005). *Post traumatic slave sydrome*. Joy DrGruy Publications.

Dickens, C. (2007). *A tale of two cities*. Signet Classics.

Dugger, C. W. (2010, November 22). Campus that apartheid ruled faces a policy rift. *The New York Times*. Retrieved from https://www.nytimes.com/2010/11/23/world/ africa/23safrica.html

Dyson, A. H., & Smitherman, G. (2009). *The right (write) start: African American language and the discourse of sounding right*. Retrieved from https://www.tcrecord.org/ content.asp?contentid=15228

Eaton, S. (2012, February). *One nation indivisible.* Retrieved from
https://www.onenationindivisible.org

Elaine, G. (2018). *The need to tackle segregation head-on.* The Long Island Index.

Eligon, J. (2015, August 9). An indelible Black-and-White line. *The New York Times,*
pp. 1, 18–19.

Eligon, J., & Gebeloff, R. (2016, August 21). Segregation, the neighbor that won't leave.
The New York Times, pp. 1, 12–13.

Ellison, R. (1995). *Invisible man.* Vintage International.

Evers, W. M. (2015, December 9). How Woodrow Wilson shut the door on K-12 education for African-Americans. *Education Week,* pp. 20–23.

Flatow, S. M. (2019, January 18). The 'apartheid' wall that isn't. *The Jewish Star,* p. 7.

Flournoy, C. (2012). Reporting race in the 21st century. *Poverty and Race, 21*(4), 3–8.

Foderaro, L. (2016, April 24). Strides, if not a solution, are seen in a housing bias suit on
long Island. *The New York Times,* pp. 1, 17.

Freire, P. (1992). *Pedagogy of hope: Reliving pedagogy of the oppressed.* Continuum.

French, D., & Simmons, W. (2015, August 26). Colorblind approaches to education are
hurting students. *Education Week,* pp. 19–21.

Galman, S., Pica-Smith, C., & Rosenberger, C. (2010). Aggressive and tender navigations: Teacher educators confront whiteness in their practice. *Journal of Teacher
Education, 61.* doi:10.1177/0022487109359776

Gates, H. L. (2016, February 7). Black America and the class divide. *The New York Times
Education Life Section,* pp. 10–11.

Gates, H. L. (2019). *Stony the road: Reconstruction, white supremacy, and the rise of Jim
Crow.* Penguin Books.

Gebrekidan, S., & Onishi, N. (2018, June 10). A tax scandal siphoning South Africa's
lifeblood. *The New York Times,* pp. 1, 12–13.

Gebrekidan, S., & Onishi, N. (2019, March 10). A battle defined by property lines and
race. *The New York Times,* pp. 1, 12–13.

Gorski, P. (2010, September 19). *So you think you're an anti-racist? Six shift of consciousness for well-intentioned White folks.* Retrieved from https://www.EDChange.org

Gould, S. J. (1983). *The mismeasure of man.* Norton.

Gregg, J. (2018). *Culturally sensitive teaching and d teachers' attitudes* (Dissertation).
Long Island University.

Gross, E. (2018). *The need to tackle segregation head-on.* Retrieved from
http://www.longislandindex.org/wp-content/uploads/2018/04/GROSS_essay_
reprint1.pdf

Hannah-Jones, N. (2014, December 21). How school segregation divides Ferguson – and
the United States. *The New York Times,* pp. 6–7.

Hannah-Jones, N. (2016, June 12). Worlds apart. *The New York Times,* pp. 34–55.

Hannah-Jones, N. (2019, July 14). It was never about busing. *The New York Times*, pp. 6–7.

Harris, A. (2012). Critical race theory. *International Encyclopedia of the Social and Behavioral Sciences*. Retrieved from http://works.bepress.com/angela_harris/17/

Haslam, R. E. (2018). Checking our biases at the door: Centering our core values in the classroom. *Literacy Today, July/August*, 24–26.

Hassan, A. (2019, August 28). Dr. King's dream speech: His son reflects on how far we have come. *The New York Times*. Retrieved from https://www.nytimes.com/2019/08/28/us/martin-luther-king-i-have-a-dream.html

Hathaway, B. (2016, September 28). *Implicit bias may help explain high preschool expulsion rates for Black children*. Retrieved from https://medicine.yale.edu/childstudy/zigler/news-article/13500/

Hirsch, E. D. (1989). *Cultural literacy*. Schwartz Pub.

Hobbs, A. (2018, September 2). Summer road-tripping While Black. *The New York Times*, p. 3.

Ingber, S., & Martin, R. (2019, August 13). *Immigration chief: 'Give me your tired, your poor who can stand on their own 2 feet'*. Retrieved from https://www.npr.org/2019/08/13/750726795/immigration-chief-give-me-your-tired-your-poor-who-can-stand-on-their-own-2-feet

Jansen, J. D. (2009). On the clash of martyrological memories. *Perspectives in Education, 27*(2), 147–157.

Johnson, R. W. (2015). *How long will South Africa survive? The looming crisis*. Jonathan Ball.

Kathrada, A. (n.d.). *Anti-Racism Network South Africa (ARNSA)*. Retrieved from https://www.arnsa.org.za/home

Kim, E. T. (2016, June 20). So Ghetto. *The Nation, 302*(25&26), 50–53.

Kimball, S. (2019, July 27). *Trump calls Baltimore a 'disgusting, rat and rodent infested mess' in attack on Rep*. Elijah Cummings. Retrieved from https://www.howardcountymd.gov/About-HoCo

Kimmelman, M. (2015, August 16). 'We figure out the city or we fail'. *The New York Times*, pp. 1, 16–17.

King, M. L. (1963). *Letter from a Birmingham Jail April 16, 1963*. Retrieved from https://www.africa.upenn.edu/Articles_Gen/Letter_Birmingham.html

King, M. L. (1967). *Chaos or community?* Hodder and Stoughton.

King, M. L. (2016). *The radical king* (C. West, Ed.). Beacon Press.

King, M. L. (n.d.). *Exclusive: Newly discovered 1964 MLK speech on civil rights, segregation & apartheid South Africa*. Retrieved from https://www.democracynow.org/2015/1/19/exclusive_newly_discovered_1964_mlk_speech

Kirkland, D. E. (2010). "Black skin, White masks": Normalizing whiteness and the trouble with the achievement gap. *Teachers College Record*. Retrieved from https://www.tcrecord.org/content.asp?contentid=16116

Kirp, D. L. (2012, May 20). Making schools work. *The New York Times*.

Koko, K. (2019, January 3). *Private school learners inch closer to the magical 100% pass rate.* Retrieved from https://www.iol.co.za/the-star/news/private-school-learners-inch-closer-to-the-magical-100-pass-rate-18674104

Kristof, N. (2014, August 31). When whites just don't get it. *The New York Times*, p. 11.

Ladson-Billings, G. (2012). Through a glass darkly: The persistence of race in educational research & scholarship. *Educational Researcher, 41*(4), 115–120.

Landsman, J. (2014, June). *Overcoming the challenges of poverty.* Retrieved from http://www.ascd.org/publications/educational-leadership/jun14/vol71/num09/Overcoming-the-Challenges-of-Poverty.aspx

Lareau, A., Weininger, E. B., & Cox, A. B. (2018, June 24). How entitled parents hurt schools. *The New York Times*.

Lawrence-Lightfoot, S. (2016, April). *American educational research association annual conference.* Keynote presented at the AERA, Washington, DC.

Lee, E., Menkart, D., & Okazawa-Rey, M. (Eds.). (2002). *Beyond heroes and holidays: A practical guide to K-12 anti-racist multicultural education and staff development.* Teaching for Change.

Lee, H. (1961). *To kill a mockingbird.* Harper & Row.

Lehohla, P. J. (2013). *Social profile of vulnerable groups 2002–2012.* Statistics South Africa. Retrieved from http://citeseerx.ist.psu.edu/viewdoc/download?doi=10.1.1.691.4270&rep=rep1&type=pdf

Lehohla, P. J. (2018). Whither a democratic dividend South Africa: The overton window of political possibilities. In M. Nassen Smith (Ed.), *Confronting inequality/the South African crisis* (pp. 106–128). Fanele.

Lester, N. A. (2011). Straight talk about the N-word. *Teaching Tolerance,* 45–48.

Lewis, S. (2019, April 25). The racial bias built into photography. *The New York Times*. Retrieved from https://www.nytimes.com/2019/04/25/lens/sarah-lewis-racial-bias-photography.html

Lockwood, B. (2020, January 30). *The history of redlining.* Retrieved from https://www.thoughtco.com/redlining-definition-4157858

Lukes, R., & Bangs, J. (2014). A critical Analysis of anti-discrimination law and microaggressions in academia. *Research in Higher Education Journal, 24.* doi:https://files.eric.ed.gov/fulltext/EJ1064084.pdf

Lynn, M., Bacon, J. N., Totten, T. L., Bridges, T. L., & Jennings, M. E. (2010). Examining teachers' beliefs about African American male students in a low-performing high school in an African American school district. *Teachers College Record, 112*(1), 289–330.

Maier, T., & Choi, A. (2017, October 22). Numbers show racial disparity. *Newsday*, pp. 2, 3, 10–12.

Mandela, N. (1964, April). Pretoria. *The Guardian*. Retrieved from https://www.theguardian.com/world/2007/apr/23/nelsonmandela

Mandela, N. (1994). *Long walk to freedom*. Little, Brown and Company.

Mbunyuza-de Heer Menlah, M. N. (2010). *Relationship between education and poverty*. University of South Africa.

McIntosh, P. (1988). *White privilege: Unpacking the invisitble knapsack*. Retrieved from https://nationalseedproject.org/Key-SEED-Texts/white-privilege-unpacking-the-invisible-knapsack

McKaiser, E. (2012, February 15). *Not White enough, not Black enough*. Retrieved from https://www.academia.edu/31520773/Not_White_Enough_Not_Black_Enough

McKaiser, E. (2015). *Run racist run*. Johannesburg: Bookstorm.

McKenzie, K., & Scheurich, J. (2004). Equity traps: A useful construct for preparing principals to lead school that are successful with racially diverse students. *Educational Administration Quarterly, 40*, 601–632.

Mercil, M. (2009, February 10). *The sunglass analogy – What do you see in the D.R.* Retrieved from http://yarari.blogspot.com/2009/02/sunglass-analogy-what-do-you-see-in-dr.html

Mervosh, S. (2018, June 25). "Why do you hate us?' He asked. 'Because you're Mexicans" she replied. *The New York Times*. Retrieved from https://www.nytimes.com/2018/06/25/us/video-diatribe-mexicans.html

Mickelson, R. A. (2011). *Exploring the school-housing nexus: A synthesis of social science Evidence* (pp. 5–8). Poverty and Research Action Council.

Mindell, A. (1995). *Sitting in the fire*. Lao Tse Press.

Moll, L. C. (2010). Mobilizing culture, language, and educational practices: Fulfilling the promises of Mendez and Brown. *Educational Researcher, 39*(6), 451–460.

Morris, W. (2017, December 24). The seer. *The New York Times Magazine*, pp. 28–33, 57.

Motlanthe, K. N. (2018). *The inequality danger: The imperative to normalise freedom confronting inequality/the South African crisis* (M. N. Smith, Ed.). Fanele.

Muhammad, K. G. (2017, January 14). No racial barrier to break (Except all of them). *The New York Times*. Retrieved from https://www.nytimes.com/2017/01/14/opinion/sunday/president-obama-martin-luther-king-racial-barrier.html

Mullainathan, S. (2015, January 4). The measuring sticks of racial bias. *The New York Times*, p. 6.

Myrdal, G. (1946). *An American dilemma: The negro problem and modern democracy*. Harper and Brothers.

Nwaubani, A. T. (2014, November 28). Who are African books for? *The New York Times*.

Obama, B. (2013, December). *President Obama delivers a eulogy for Nelson Mandela*. Johannesburg. Retrieved from https://www.npr.org/sections/thetwo-way/2013/12/10/249935322/listen-president-obama-delivers-a-eulogy-for-nelson-mandela

Olson, R. A. (1992). *White privilege in schools*. Retrieved from http://www.schtools.com/membersnew/documents/MSSAA/LLP15-16_CPL_WhitePrivilege.pdf

Oneale, L. (2013, December 15). South Africa a failing democracy: Hendrik Verwoerd, Jeff Radeba and Pik Botha. *Liberty Voice.* Retrieved from https://guardianlv.com/2013/12/south-africa-a-failing-democracy-hendrik-verwoerd-jeff-radebe-and-pik-botha/

Onishi, N. (2016, August 14). Police struggle to gain trust of apartheid's victims. *The New York Times,* pp. 6, 9.

Onishi, N. (2019, May 5). South African voters are kept in dark on who is financing campaigns. *The New York Times,* p. 10.

Onishi, S., & Gebrekidan, S. (2018, August 5). Amassing power in South Africa as corruption rots its schools. *The New York Times,* pp. 1, 10–11.

Overcoming the Challenges of Poverty. (2014). *Educational Leadership, 71,* 16–21.

Paine, T. (2019). *Common sense.* BLURB.

Painter, N. I. (2019, April 28). After reconstruction. *The New York Times Book Review,* p. 14.

Pariona, A. (2019, July 18). *WorldAtlas.* Retrieved from https://www.worldatlas.com/articles/ethnic-makeup-of-south-africa.html

Parker, M. (2019). *Magical negro.* Tin House Books.

Paton, A. (2002). *Cry, the beloved country.* Vintage.

Payne, R. K. (2013). *Framework for understanding poverty.* Aha! Process.

PIRLS International Results in Reading. (2016). Retrieved from http://timssandpirls.bc.edu/pirls2016/international-results/pirls/student-achievement/pirls-achievement-results/

Polgreen, L. (2013, September 16). Trading privilege for privation, family hits a nation's nerve. *The New York Times.*

Randall, D. (n.d.). *The Black poets.* Bantam.

Rosales, J. (n.d.). *The racist beginnings of standardized testing.* Retrieved from http://www.nea.org/home/73288.htm

Ross, A. (2018, April 30). How American racism influenced Hitler. *The New Yorker.*

Rothstein, R. (2008). Whose problem is poverty? *Educational Leadership,* 8–13.

Roy, Y. (2019, November 26). Bill would target prejudice. *Newsday,* p. A4.

Rutenberg, J. (2015, August 2). Overcome. *The New York Times,* pp. 31–48.

Ryzik, M. (2016, May 22). 'Roots' for a new era. *The New York Times.*

Schroeder, F. (2015, November 14). Everything is in extremes in Masiphumelele, says school principal. *Weekend Argus,* p. 10.

Schuster, D. (2016, October 2). The tale of two New York cities. *The New York Post,* pp. 24–25.

Selfa, L. (2010, October 21). *The roots of racism.* Retrieved from https://socialistworker.org/2010/10/21/the-roots-of-racism

Shabalala, N. (2018). Feeling some Typ'a way: A young Black woman's experience of education in South Africa. *South African Journal of Higher Education, 32*(4), 215–228.

Shen, F. (2018, October 20). *A walk with the mayor through Sandtown after a spike in shootings.* Retrieved from https://baltimore.citybizlist.com/article/507848/a-walk-with-the-mayor-through-sandtown-after-a-spike-in-shootings

Sokolower, J. (2011). Schools and the new Jim Crow: An interview with Michelle Alexander. *Rethinking Schools, 26*(2), 13–17.

Solar, I. I. (2013, June 16). The picture of a tragic event that changed South Africa's history. *Digital Journal.* Retrieved from http://www.digitaljournal.com/article/352398

Spaull, N. (2015, November 8). While the rich get education, SA's poor get just 'schooling'. *Sunday Times*, p. 21.

Spaull, N. (2017, December 5). *The unfolding reading crisis: The new PIRLS 2016 results.* Retrieved from https://nicspaull.com/2017/12/05/the-unfolding-reading-crisis-the-new-pirls-2016-results/

Staples, B. (2016, January 10). A 'most dangerous' newspaper. *The New York Times Book Review*, p. 12.

Staples, B. (2018, July 28). How the suffrage movement betrayed Black women. *New York Times.* Retrieved from https://www.nytimes.com/2018/07/28/opinion/sunday/suffrage-movement-racism-black-women.html

Stengel, R. (2008, July 9). Mandela: His 8 lessons of leadership. *Time.* Retrieved from http://content.time.com/time/subscriber/article/0,33009,1821659-2,00.html

Stevenson, B. (2015). *Just Mercy.* Spiegel & Grau.

Style, E. (1996). Curriculum as window & mirror. *Social Science Record*, 35–38.

Subreenduth, S. (2013). Theorizing social justice ambiguities in an era of neoliberalism: The case of post-apartheid South Africa. *Educational Theory, 63*(6), 581–600.

Sulla, V., & Zikhali, P. (2018). *Overcoming poverty and inequality in South Africa: An assessment of drivers, constraints and opportunities.* The World Bank. Retrieved from http://documents.worldbank.org/curated/en/530481521735906534/pdf/124521-REV-OUO-South-Africa-Poverty-and-Inequality-Assessment-Report-2018-FINAL-WEB.pdf

Taylor, E., Gillborn, D., & Ladson-Billings, G. (Eds.). (2009). *Foundations of critical race theory in education.* Routledge.

Tefera, A., Frankenberg, E., Siegel-Hawley, G., & Chirichigno, G. (2011). *Integrating suburban schools: How to benefit from growing diversity and avoid segregation.* The Civil Rights Project.

Turner, E. O. (2015). Districts' responses to demographic change: Making sense of race, class, and immigration in political and organizational context. *American Educational Research Journal, 52*(1), 4–39.

Turton, J. (2017, June 2). *'Ghetto tourism': New York's disturbing new trend.* Retrieved from https://www.dazeddigital.com/artsandculture/article/36160/1/ghetto-tourism-new-yorks-disturbing-new-trend

Tversky, A., & Kahneman, D. (1974). Judgment under certainty: Heuristics and biases. *Science/New Series, 185*, 1124–1131.

Urban Institute: Nine Charts about Wealth Inequality in America (Updated). (2017, October 5). Retrieved from http://apps.urban.org/features/wealth-inequality-charts/

Vox, L. (2019, July 3). *The origins of Black history month*. Retrieved from https://www.thoughtco.com/origins-of-black-history-month-p2-45346

Warren, M. (2010). *Fire in the heart: How White activists embrace racial justice*. Oxford University Press.

Weir, K. (2016, November). Inequality at school. *Monitor on Psychology*, 43–47.

Weiss, E. (2014, December 1). *Stop counting on educational miracles/policymakers who proclaim miraculous progress in education don't usually have their facts straight*. Retrieved from https://www.usnews.com/topics/author/elaine-weiss

Wells, A. S. (2009). *Why boundaries matter: A study of five separate and unequal long Island school districts*. Final report to the Long Island Index. Teachers College, Center for Understanding Race and Education (CURE). Retrieved from https://new.every1graduates.org/why-boundaries-matter-a-study-of-five-separate-and-unequal-long-island-school-districts/

West, C. (2005). The new cultural politics of difference. In C. McCarthy, W. Crichlow, G. Dimitriadis, & N. Dolby (Eds.), *Race, identity, and representation in education* (pp. 29–41). Routledge.

Wilde, O. (2007). *The epigrams of Oscar Wilde*. Wordsworth.

Wilkerson, I. (2015, July 19). Our racial moment of truth. *The New York Times*, p. 4.

Williams, T. C. (2018, June 27). Adrian Piper's show at MoMA is the largest ever for a living artist. Why hasn't she seen it? *The New York Times*. Retrieved from https://www.nytimes.com/2018/06/27/magazine/adrian-pipers-self-imposed-exile-from-america-and-from-race-itself.html

Willingham, D. T. (2017, November 25). How to get your mind to read. *The New York Times*.

Woodson, J. (2014). *Brown girl dreaming*. Puffin Books.

Index

Printed in the United States
By Bookmasters